A Pictorial HISTORY OF THE B-2A SPIRIT STEALTH BOMBER

Jim Goodall

FOREWORD BY Dr. John Cashen
"FATHER OF THE B-2"

4880 Lower Valley Road • Atglen, PA 19310

Library of Congress Control Number: 2016933926

Designed by Justin Watkinson
Type set in Agency FB/Univers LT Std
ISBN: 978-0-7643-5075-7
Printed in China

Published by Schiffer Publishing, Ltd.
4880 Lower Valley Road
Atglen, PA 19310
Phone: (610) 593-1777; Fax: (610) 593-2002
E-mail: Info@schifferbooks.com
Web: www.schifferbooks.com

Dedication

For my Sweet Woman, Rosemary Cox Goodall, the best wife a man could ever hope for; she loves airplanes, she's a good editor, loves going to air shows, riding on the back of my Harley, loves to dance, I love her extended family, her friends who are now my friends and the most important aspect of our marriage, she makes me laugh every day.

Contents

Acknowledgments

Without the help of those listed, I would have been out of luck putting the book together.

Patrick Joyce
Northrop Grumman Systems Corporation
Corporate Intellectual Asset Management

Brooks McKinney, APR
Communications Fellow
Northrop Grumman Aerospace Systems

Todd Kabalan, TSgt, USAF
Secretary of the Air Force National Media Engagement Office

Michael Lombardi
Corporate Historian, The Boeing Company

Candy Knight
Deputy Chief, Public Affairs
509th Bomb Wing, Whiteman AFB, Missouri

Captain John M. Cooper
Chief, Public Affairs, 509th Bomb Wing

Captain Spencer Wartman, Spirit #568 (509BW)
Major Tim "Bling" Rezac, Spirit #343 (131BW)

Dock Tour (all Airmen from the 13th Aircraft Maintenance Unit, 509th Aircraft Maintenance Squadron)
– Senior Airman Gavin Anderson
– Senior Airman Ryan Ream
– Airman 1st Class Clint Cox
– Staff Sgt. Alex Salazar
– Senior Airman Giacomo Restivo
– Senior Airman Ian Linker
– Staff Sgt. Joshua Mesulit
– Staff Sgt. Lee Smith-Whaley
– Staff Sgt. David Humphery

Life Support (parachute shop)
– Tech Sgt. Manuel Bocanegra, 509th Operations Support Squadron

Weapons Load Trainer, 509th Maintenance Group, Weapons Standardization section
– Staff Sgt. Corey Carlson
– Senior Airman Charles Balog
– Senior Airman Derek Asbury

509th Operations Support Squadron Weather Flight
– Senior Airman Nathaniel Dean
– Senior Airman Christopher Steward

Don Logan
Tony Monetti
Harry Foster
Frank Cavuoti
Randy Koivisto
Jesse Lazano
Michael Schratt
James P. Stevenson

Capt. Jose R. Surita, jr.
Commandant of Cadets
Air Force ROTC – Det 925
University of Wisconsin – Madison

The men and women of the 509th Bomb Wing that keep the "Beast" in the air protecting America's interests worldwide.

And my wife, Rosemary.

Foreword

Rightfully, the first picture in this history is of John K. Northrop, known to all his co-workers as Jack. Six months before he passed away, in 1981, and after he saw an early scale model of what would become the B-2A Spirit, he is quoted as saying: "Now I know why God has kept me alive over the past twenty-five years."

Jack had believed that an all flying wing aircraft was the closest that man could replicate bird in flight. He was devastated when, in 1950, the USAF canceled his YB-49 bomber and destroyed all the aircraft built or in fabrication. He then made sure nearly all the drawings and technical data were also destroyed. He retired from aviation at age fifty-seven never again to work on any airplane. He was a true aviation pioneer whose name had never appeared on the Collier Trophy. That was until in 1992 when the USAF and Northrop Corp. team received the award for the B-2A design and development. I, for one, believed that Jack's dream had been vindicated that night.

The idea for the B-2 started in 1979 with operational and survivability analysis which revealed that a flying wing having the radar cross section and other observables demonstrated during the already on-going Tacit Blue could survive, unrefueled at high altitude, against the most capable integrated air defense expected anywhere in the world during its lifetime. It would simply be a replacement for the venerable B-52. The analysis also showed just what kind of aircraft shape would be optimum. As a result the first planform "sketch" looks amazingly like the B-2 of today, except we quickly found that six F-18 engines could be substituted with four being developed for B-1B.

Very few who worked on the B-2A ever worked on the YB-49. There was no corporate memory and little technical data to draw upon when we looked for it. The B-2 has no heritage except the Northrop name. We all knew that that a flying wing had been a design option for decades. The B-2 is an original design.

Tacit Blue was crucial for the new bomber, although it was not a large flying wing, but a classic small wing-body-tail. It demonstrated a new way to design stealth, moving away from the faceted approach of the F-117 and towards three dimensional curvature and planform alignment. This approach helped mitigate the big difference in size and that was never an important issue. The successful Tacit Blue test program of 135 flights was critical to the risk reduction required for the bomber's new approach to stealth.

Those who saw the YB-49 fly by in 1949 recall an almost mystical feeling of seeing the future, something they never forgot. Many today seeing the B-2A have the same feeling. It has also been characterized as "aircraft as art." Air Force pilots often say; "if it looks good it must fly good." The USAF expects to keep it operational well past 2050. I would suggest that longevity is the best measure of an aircraft "goodness."

I would like to recognize my co-designer, Irv Waaland and Northrop' development program manager, Jim Kinnu. I would also like to congratulate the great Northrop team that developed and built the "JET" and the Northrop Grumman team that continues to help "keep 'em flying." I would also like to salute the USAF SPO team under Gen. Richard Schofield and the men who have served in the 509th for making it "America's Airplane." I commend you to enjoy the most comprehensive picture history yet of the B-2A.

Dr. John Cashen,
B-2 designer

Introduction

Whiteman Air Force Base

Home of the 509th Bomb Wing

America's Air Force No One Comes Close

This Certificate presented to

MSgt. (Ret) James Christian Goodall, USAF

on the occasion of his B-2 Simulator Ride

in

SMB-2-001 (WST-3), the Spirit of Warrensburg

on Wednesday, 4 June 2014

Flown as SPIRIT01, takeoff time was 2000Z, land time was 2200Z, with a flight duration of 2.0 hours. Mid-air refueling was accomplished with a KC-135R, Turbo 42 from the 131 ARW, Offutt AFB ANG, along AR110E, on-loading 10,000 pounds of JP-8 fuel at an altitude of 25,000 feet. Mission was conducted in the skies above Whiteman AFB, St. Louis, and Kansas City Missouri.

Congratulations - keep the Spirit flying high!

Captain Spencer G. Wartman, Spirit #568, B-2 Pilot

When I started this B-2 book project back in November 1988, I wasn't quite sure where it would take me or how long the journey would be. My goal was to put something down in print that would show the world just how innovative the American aerospace industry is when they put their collective heads together to create Jack Northrop's dream come true, the B-2A Spirit Stealth Bomber.

I figured that I would be hindered by the very same mindset that surrounded the original Blackbird program: Cygnus to Senior Crown. The Blackbird's unofficial/official policy toward the release of photos and information back in the late 1960s, through the end of the program in 1990, was not to cooperate, drag their feet on my FOIA requests, and just make life as difficult as they could in my quest for information.

While stationed at the Pentagon during Desert Storm, I had the opportunity to challenge the then Deputy Director for Program Security for Special Projects, Pete Eames, as to why I was being denied the information that I requested on the Blackbirds and F-117 programs, when in fact the information I was requesting was never classified. His response was: "That's just policy."

Fast forward to February 2014. After receiving the go-ahead from the Air Force media office, I contacted the Northrop Grumman Corporation (NG) with my request for photos and documentation on the B-2, as well as the early Northrop flying wings: the XB-35 and YB-49. Much to my delight, Brooks McKinney and Pat Joyce of Northrop Grumman's corporate public relations and media relations departments replied that they would help anyway they could with releasable images as long as NG received photo credit.

At Whiteman AFB, the wing's PAO, Capt. John Cooper, set the ball rolling once the crew at the Air Force's public affairs office for book support gave the "thumbs up" to support this book.

As the title states, *A Pictorial History of the B-2A Spirit*, the book has limited text but fully captioned photos and drawings. There are over 500 images, with a large number of photos and drawings that have never been published until now.

As with the F-117, and in some regards, my dealings with the SR-71 community, I knew that with anything associated with a classified program such as the B-2A Spirit, that I would have to deal with all of the security issues that one has to deal with when one is pursuing the "unknown." During my two-day photo shoot, not only did the 509th Bomb Wing team at Whiteman roll out the red carpet, allowing me to photograph on the flight line and in the dedicated individual hangars, they allowed me to see, but not shoot, heavy maintenance being performed on the *Spirit of Florida* and *Spirit of Pennsylvania*. Thinking it just couldn't get any better, our final stop, and totally unknown to me, was one that I never in a million years thought I would experience: over two hours flying the B-2 simulator.

I hope you enjoy my efforts to show the world the B-2A Spirit in a different and brighter light.

The Early Years at Hawthorne

TOP LEFT: John (Jack) Knudsen Northrop Inventor/Industrialist 1895–1981.

Jack Northrop formed Northrop Aircraft, Inc. in 1939, and built the first successful N-1M flying wing and the XP-56 flying wing fighter. He created the first US rocket-powered aircraft, the JB-10 flying bomb, the P-61 Black Widow night fighter, and the XP-79 flying wing fighter.

After the war, he founded the Northrop Institute of Technology and completed the XB-35 flying wing bomber. He later built the jet-propelled XB-49 flying wing bomber, the X-4 research plane, and the Snark, America's first inertial-guided intercontinental ballistic missile. *Northrop Grumman*

TOP RIGHT: In the late 1940s, color photography was not very common so it is rare that we get to see such a great bottom view of the Northrop XB-35. *Northrop Grumman*

TOP LEFT: On June 25, 1946, the XB-35 flying wing took-off from the runway at the Northrop Aircraft Co. and made its maiden flight to Edwards AFB (then Muroc Army Air Field). *Northrop Grumman*

BOTTOM LEFT: A Northrop YB-49 is serviced in preparation for a test flight at Muroc Army Air Field. *Northrop Grumman*

TOP RIGHT: Looking down the length of one of Northrop's magnificent flying wings, the eight engine YB-49A. *Northrop Grumman*

MIDDLE RIGHT: Aerial view of a Northrop XB-35 over what appears to be Rogers Dry Lake, part of the Muroc Army Air Field flight test complex. *Northrop Grumman*

BOTTOM RIGHT: A view of an YB-49 taken just before taxiing to the runway for another test flight. *Northrop Grumman*

TOP LEFT: A rear view of a Northrop YB-49 as it flies over Rogers Dry Lake. Unlike today's jet engines, 1940s vintage jets were grossly underpowered and lacked reliability, hence the need for eight engines versus four on the B-2A Spirit. *Northrop Grumman*

TOP RIGHT: A frontal view of a Northrop YB-49 over Rogers Dry Lake with Muroc Army Air Field in the background. *Northrop Grumman*

BOTTOM RIGHT: A rare color view of the bottom of a Northrop XB-35 in flight. *Northrop Grumman*

TOP LEFT: Two rivals: the Northrop YB-49 and the Boeing B-47A. The conversion of the long-range XB-35 to jet power essentially cut the effective range of the aircraft in half, putting it in the medium-range bomber category with Boeing's new swept-winged jet bomber the B-47 Stratojet. The B-47 was optimized for high-altitude and high-speed flight, and, in an era where speed and altitude were becoming the name of the game, the YB-49's thick airfoil could never be maximized for high-speed performance. *Northrop Grumman*

MIDDLE LEFT: A leap in time where we have a Boeing B-52H Stratofortress flying in formation with a Northrop Grumman B-2A Spirit flying wing. *Air Force/509th BW*

TOP RIGHT: By 1949, there was a series of complex agreements: the two XB-35s were to be scrapped; the first two YB-35s were also to be scrapped; the one remaining YB-49 was to continue in flight test; four YB-35s and three YB-35As were to be equipped with six J35-A-19 engines each, and converted to YB-35Bs for flight test; one YB-35A was to be converted into a prototype of the RB-49A and designated the YRB-49A. *Northrop Grumman*

BOTTOM LEFT: A YB-49 just after liftoff from the Northrop plant in Hawthorne, CA. What is amazing in today's world is the close proximity to the local neighborhood. *Northrop Grumman*

TOP LEFT: After September 11, 1946, the XB-35 was grounded because of the difficulties involving the gearbox and propeller-control. The aircraft had by then completed three tests, for three hours and four minutes of flight-testing. The XB-35s would manage to fly for a total of thirty-six hours, for an amortized cost of $1.8 million per hour. *Northrop Grumman*

MIDDLE LEFT: In the late 1940s, and into the early 1950s, multi-wheel landing gear was still a number of years away, hence the need for very large tires on the nose and mains on the XB-35 and the YB49s. *Northrop Grumman*

BOTTOM LEFT: A view of one of the first of two XB-35s under construction in the Northrop Aircraft plant located in Hawthorne, California. *Northrop Grumman*

TOP RIGHT: The maiden flight of the first XB-35 was made on June 25, 1946, covering the distance from Northrop field at Hawthorne to Muroc Lake. Cost of the one aircraft had been about $14,300,000 to this time in 1946 dollars. *Northrop Grumman*

BOTTOM RIGHT: All the smoke under the YB-49 is the testing of its fire suppression system effects on all eight engines. *Northrop Grumman*

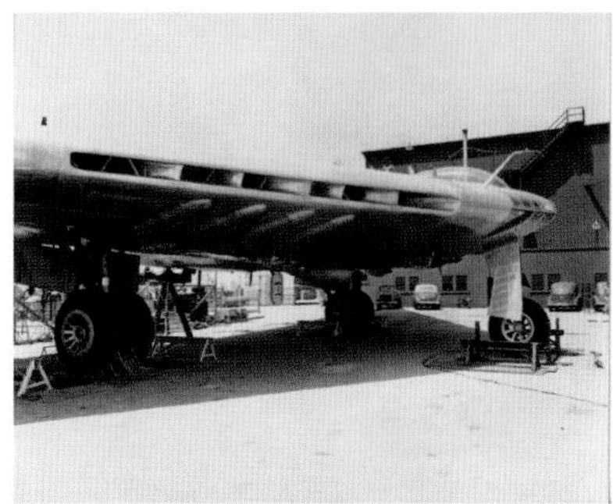

TOP LEFT: Two film crews standing on top of a couple of vintage 1947 Fords ready to document the maiden flight of the first YB-49 as it's preflighted on the northrop ramp in Hawthorne, CA. *Northrop Grumman*

MIDDLE LEFT: Looking down the trailing edge of the eight-engine YB-49. At the tip of the trailing edge tail of the YB-49 would have been 4 x .50 caliber (12.7 mm) machine guns. They were to be mounted in rotating "stinger" tail cone if the B-49A were to become a production aircraft. *Northrop Grumman*

BOTTOM LEFT: The leading edge of the YB-49 was made up mostly of air intakes for its eight Allison/General Electric J35-A-5s. *Northrop Grumman*

TOP RIGHT: Among the aircraft later completed were two airframes that the Air Force ordered be fitted with jet propulsion and designated as YB-49s. The first of these new YB-49 jet-powered aircraft flew on October 21, 1947, and immediately proved more promising than its piston-engine counterpart. The YB-49 set an unofficial endurance record of staying continually above 40,000ft (12,200m) for 6.5 hours. *Northrop Grumman*

LEFT: Northrop had never before built such large aircraft, and lacked the facilities to do so. Most assembly had to take place outdoors. *Northrop Grumman*

TOP RIGHT: The complex system of huge counter-rotating propellers never worked satisfactorily, and doomed the XB-35s to failure. *Northrop Grumman*

UPPER MIDDLE RIGHT: The cockpit of the Northrop YB-49. What is not shown is the flight engineer's station with the engine controls for the eight Allison/General Electric J35-A-5 jet engines that powered the YB-49. *Northrop Grumman*

LOWER MIDDLE RIGHT: A very large bubble canopy on the XB-35s and the YB-49s gave the pilot a commanding view of his world. *Northrop Grumman*

BOTTOM RIGHT: A telegram from Air Materiel Command dated January 11, 1949, formally told Northrop the bad news: "the contractor is directed to stop all work authorized … with the exception of the engineering, fabrication, and flight test applicable to the YRB-49A airplane." Shortly after the cancellation, all of the Northrop flying wings were destroyed. *Northrop Grumman*

LEFT: In this view at the Northrop plant in Hawthorne, CA, are four of Jack Nothrop's flying wings: closest is a YB-49A (42-102367), while in the background still under construction is an XB-35 directly above the YB-49A, and a second YB-49 is on the extreme left side of the photo. *Northrop Grumman*

TOP RIGHT: In a hangar at Edwards AFB, one of two XB-35s, and two of the Northrop N-1Ms. There are only two of the early Northrop flying wings existing today: one, N-9M, is owned and flown by Planes of Fame in Chino, CA, and the other is on display at the Udvar-Hazy Center in Chantilly, Virginia, at the National Air & Space Museum, the companion facility to the Air & Space Museum in Washington, DC. *Northrop Grumman*

BOTTOM RIGHT: Jack Northrop leaning on the nose of one of his N-1Ms having a word with the Northrop test pilot Moye Stephens, as the plane rests on Rogers Dry Lake at Muroc AAF, now Edwards AFB, CA. *Northrop Grumman*

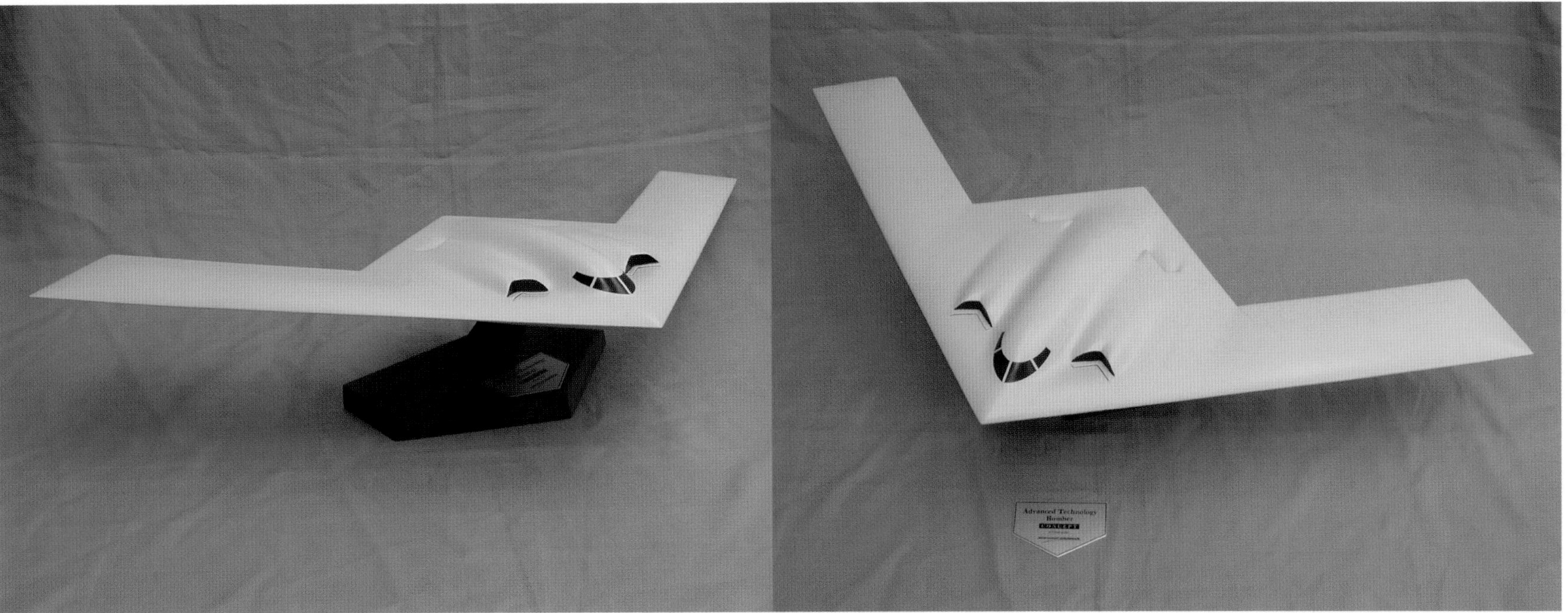

TOP: The evolution of what was called the ATB, or "Advance Technology Bomber," as the B-2A began to take on its now very familiar shape. The original version was to fly only at high altitude and did not have the need for control at low levels. The design for the operational B-2As has five trailing edge points, where the early design only had three. *Northrop Grumman*

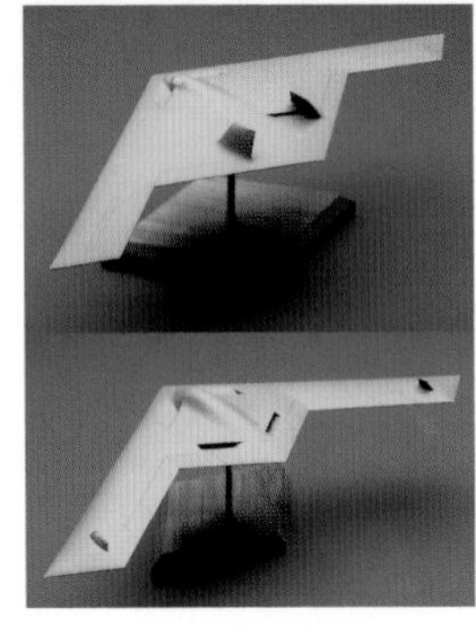

BOTTOM LEFT: A B-2A with vertical tails was one of the options considered for slow speed directional control. On the operational B-2A Spirit, the landing gear doors act a vertical control surfaces at slow speeds. *Northrop Grumman*

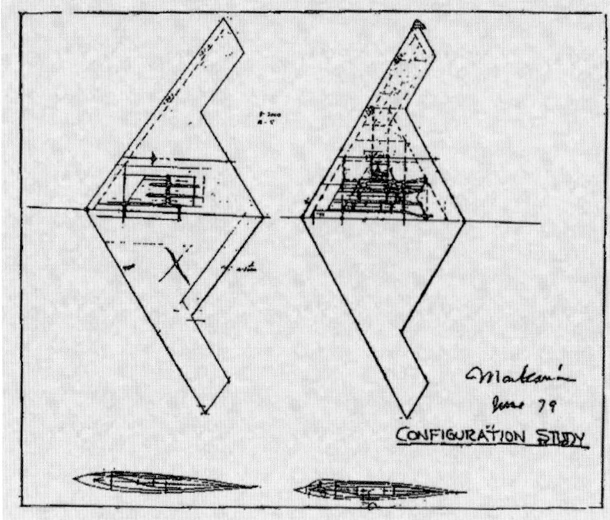

BOTTOM RIGHT: The first hand-drawn sketch of what became the B-2A on this piece of parchment paper dated June 1979. *Northrop Grumman*

Tacit Blue: The B-2 Technology Demonstrator

The Northrop Tacit Blue was a technology demonstrator aircraft created to demonstrate a low observable, stealth surveillance aircraft with a low probability of intercept radar and other sensors. The Tacit Blue (a.k.a. Shamu, or the Whale) program actually had started in 1978 as part of an overall secret Air Force effort called Pave Mover. Northrop worked under a sole-source, $136 million contract. In time, test and support expenses pushed the total Whale cost to $165 million. *Northrop Grumman*

TOP AND MIDDLE BOTTOM: In developing any new aircraft, be it a flight test article or an operational system, the cockpit needs the attention of the men who were charged in flying it for the first time. A lot of time and effort is put into the location of all controls and instruments required for a safe flight. *Northrop Grumman*

BOTTOM LEFT AND RIGHT: A Northrop flight test engineer sits in the cockpit mockup with paper instruments to ensure that all of the necessary instruments and flight controls are all within easy reach and visible to the test pilot. *Northrop Grumman*

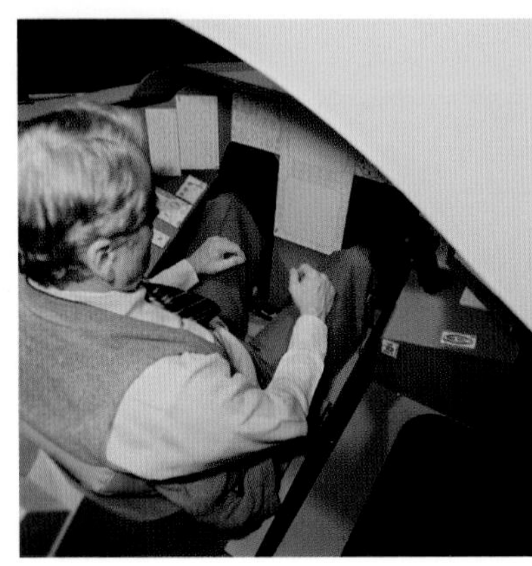

Northrop Grumman RCS Facility

This view is one of two outdoor radar test ranges operated by aerospace companies in the Antelope Valley. The Tejon Test Site is a remote test facility and is owned and operated by the Northrop Grumman Corporation. It encompasses over 1,400 acres, and is self-contained and self-sufficient. Its primary function is to conduct electromagnetic testing utilizing two outdoor Radar Cross Section (RCD) ranges, two outdoor antenna ranges, and one indoor RCS Compact range. This secure facility is operated by Northrop Grumman and was built in the mid 1980s to pursue the development of Stealth technologies. *Author's collection*

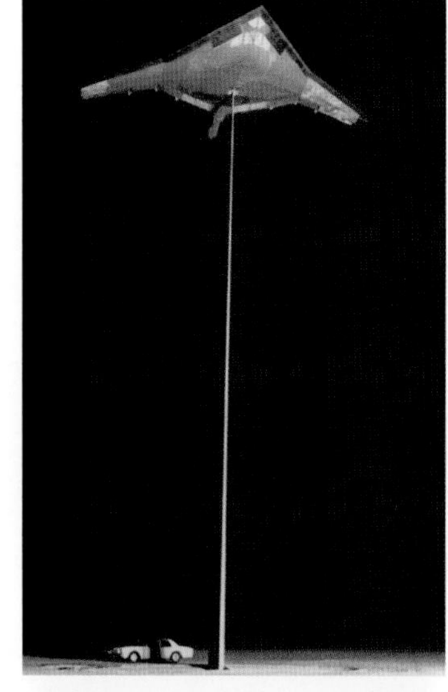

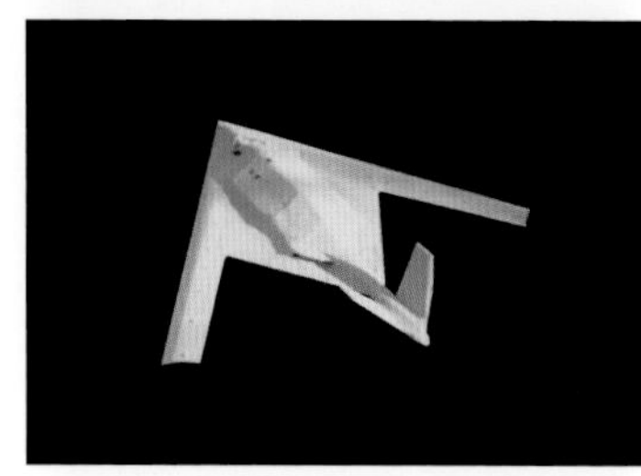

TOP LEFT: In 1991, Scaled Composites, now part of Northrop Grumman, built a four-tenths scale RCS model of the final configuration of the B-2A and secured it on the pole at RATSCAT located in the White Sands Proving Grounds, near Holloman AFB, NM. *Northrop Grumman*

BOTTOM LEFT: The array of radars used to evaluate the radar cross-section of the test subject at the Tejon Ranch RCS facility. *Author's collection*

TOP AND MIDDLE RIGHT: The only known images of the Lockheed Martin ATB proposal, code-named Senior Peg, on the RCS pole at the Helendale RCS facility. *Lockheed via Joseph Jones*

BOTTOM RIGHT: Inside the enclosed RCS facility at the Lockheed Martin Helendale RCS facility, the Northrop Grumman X-47B is readied for testing. *Lockheed Martin*

A long exposure of the Scaled Composites four-tenths sized B-2A on the RCS pole at the Northrop Grumman Tejon Ranch RCS facility. *Northrop Grumman*

Escape System Testing

In testing the B-2As escape system, a structurally identical cockpit had to be built and the ejection seats were tested to ensure a safe and reliable escape system in the unlikely event the crew had to eject from the aircraft. It worked as planned as the *Spirit of Kansas*, AV-12, was lost on takeoff on February 23, 2008, at Andersen AFB, Guam. *Bill Norris*

B-2 Spirit Functional Iron Bird System Test Rig

Prior to the start of fabrication and assembly of the B-2A Spirit, a fully functional system had to be developed to ensure that all of the various mechanical systems worked in coordination with one another. An "Iron Bird" structure was built incorporating all of the primary flight controls, systems, and subsystems. *Northrop Grumman*

B-2 Spirit Production Begins

LEFT: A view looking down a row of B-2As at Air Force Plant 42, Site 4. The B-2A closest to the front of the line is AV-5, the *Spirit of Ohio*. The Site 4 facility was designed for a production run of 133 B-2s, but in the end, only twenty-one were produced along with two static airframes. *Northrop Grumman*

TOP RIGHT: As with all major weapons systems, if the B-2 were to go back into production or that major structural parts need to be re-manufactured, the B-2s production fixtures are stored at Davis Monthan AFB in MASDC, better known as the "Bone Yard." *Author's collection*

BOTTOM RIGHT: A satellite view of Air Force Plant 42, Site 4, the home of the B-2 production facility and now probably the Northrop Grumman LRS-B production facility—or as some have called the LRS-B, the B-3. *Author's collection*

BOEING
HUGHES
NORTHROP

OPPOSITE PAGE: This view of the B-2 production site beginning of production of the twenty-one B-2 airframes. Note "Northrop" and "SAC" badge at top right: all were gone by 1990. Once all of the B-2s were delivered to Air Force, this facility became the B-2s dedicated overhaul and modification center. *Northrop Grumman*

TOP LEFT: Looking down to the production tooling of the aft-center fuselage, this view is of assembly AV-21, the *Spirit of Louisiana,* in the foreground and assembly AV-20, the *Spirit of Pennsylvania*, the first Block 30 B-2A delivered to the Air Force, in the background. Unlike most aircraft manufacturing facilities, this Boeing production line is as quite as your office cubicle. *Boeing*

TOP RIGHT: The very last Boeing built outer wing for B-2 the *Spirit of Louisiana* is hosted overhead at Boeing's secure production facility at Boeing Field, Seattle, WA. As with the aft-center fuselage, this very long, seamless wing was transported via Lockheed C-5B to the B-2s final assembly facility at Air Force Plant 42, Site Four, Palmdale, CA. *Boeing*

LEFT: A long view of the Boeing built aft center fuselage and outer wing production location at Boeing Field. In addition to the aft center fuselage and outer wings, the LTV subsidiary built the B-2s engine nacelles and inter wing assemblies. *Boeing*

THIS PAGE AND OPPOSITE: A view looking down the B-2 production at the peak of manufacture. In the photo are AV-6 through AV-12: *the Spirit of Mississippi, Spirit of Texas, Spirit of Missouri, Spirit of California, Spirit of South Carolina, Spirit of Washington* and at the end of the line is the *Spirit of Kansas. Northrop Grumman*

LEFT: To remove all the paint and specialized coatings that had been applied to the B-2, Northrop Grumman developed a paint stripping system that utilized wheat husks that successfully removed the paint, and left the composite surfaces untouched. The job is messy and the noise of four or five bead-blasting units going full blast is truly deafening. *Northrop Grumman*

TOP LEFT: *The Spirit of America*, AV-1, s/n 82-1066, receives a fresh coat of paint as it is readied for its very first public appearance, the roll out of AV-1 on November 22,1988. *Northrop Grumman*

TOP RIGHT: The B-2s Overhaul and Depot is located at Air Force Plant 42, Site 4 and is where all B-2s go to be refreshed with new radar absorbent materials, also known as "RAM," and improved electrostatic coatings. Aircraft in the operational fleet are sent periodically to Northrop Grumman's facility in Palmdale, CA, for programmed depot maintenance (PDM) as part of an Air Force contract for overall B-2 support.

ABOVE: Due to the hazards of breathing paint dust, some of it toxic, all personnel tasked to strip or paint the B-2, or any large aircraft for that matter, must wear protective clothing. *Northrop Grumman*

RIGHT: A painter finishes up the final part of a B-2's wing. The painter is totally enclosed in an air tight paint suit with a breathable air pump via the hose attached the back of his protective head gear. *Northrop Grumman*

TOP RIGHT: Once all of the marking and stenciling is done, time to pack up your masking tape, take off your airtight top cover and head home. *Northrop Grumman*

BOTTOM LEFT AND RIGHT: Even with all of the automation used in designing and building the B-2A, it still takes the sharp eye and steady hand of the guy with the masking tape to put the final touches on the B-2A Spirit. *Northrop Grumman*

The National Museum of the Air Force B-2 Spirit

The National Museum of the Air Force has a B-2A on display, the *Spirit of Freedom.* This airframe was one of two static airframes used in the development of the B-2A. When the Air Force Museum officials were told that they would be getting one of the two static airframes they were thrilled. The only stipulation was that the museum had to have an armed guard on the exhibit twenty-four hours a day, seven days a week. The museum told them to keep their B-2A. After much discussion it was assured by the museum that no one would have access to the static B-2A and the requirement for the 24/7 guard was removed. *NMUSAF*

TOP AND BOTTOM LEFT: The National Museum of the Air Force's Northrop Grumman B-2, the *Spirit of Freedom*, during its one and only outdoor photo shoot. *NMUSAF*

RIGHT GROUP OF FOUR: These poor quality shots were taken of the B-2A Static Airframe, AV-998, as it waited to be reassembled at the NMUSAF's restoration facility in Area B of Wright Patterson AFB, OH.

Two static structural test airframe exceeded ultimate (150 percent) load test before fracture at 161 percent in December 1992. The second static airframe was dismantled and shipped to the Dayton, OH, and reassembled using non-flight, damaged, or out of specification rated external pieces and parts. *Author's collection*

PUBLIC UNVEILING OF THE SPIRIT O

Public Unveiling of the Spirit on November 22, 1988

The public unveiling of the *Spirit of America*, AV-1 (82-1066), at the Northrop B-2A Production Facility at Air Force Plant 42, Site 4, then known as "Fatal Beauty." *Northrop Grumman*

TOP LEFT: A select group of dignitaries, politicians, Air Force brass and selected members of the aerospace community were invited to the public unveiling. *Northrop Grumman*

BOTTOM LEFT: *Spirit of America* taxis to the Edwards AFB runway during early flight testing. On the rear fuselage of the B-2A is a trailing wire sensor used to calibrate the B-2A's flight performance. *Air Force/509th BW*

TOP RIGHT: *Spirit of America* on landing approach at Edwards AFB, CA, while a Northrop YF-23 "Black Widow II" waits its turn. The name "Black Widow" was killed almost as soon as it was mentioned by order of Northrop's marketing staff and senior management. *Air Force/509th BW*

BOTTOM RIGHT: The *Spirit of New York*, an "ED" coded B-2A, AV-3 (82-1068), taxis past the Edwards tower after a flyby during an airshow. *Author's collection*

TOP RIGHT: The *Spirit of Ohio*, AV-5 (82-1070), one of the five full-scale development B-2As carrying an "ED," heads to the south base at Edwards AFB during envelope expansion testing. *Air Force/509th BW*

BOTTOM LEFT: The *Spirit of America* flies over Edwards AFB during early flight testing. The trailing wire instrument structure is evident in this image and the early B-2As were used for envelope expansion, and maintenance training and were not mission-capable in the early Block 10 configuration. *Air Force/509th BW*

BOTTOM CENTER: The *Spirit of America* off the coast of California near Vandenberg AFB with the trailing wire sensor extended and extreme condensation formed on the top of the engine inlets. *Air Force/509th BW*

BOTTOM RIGHT: The *Spirit of Mississippi*, AV-6 (82-1071), during its first flight with landing gear extended. Edwards AFB is in the background. *Air Force/509th BW*

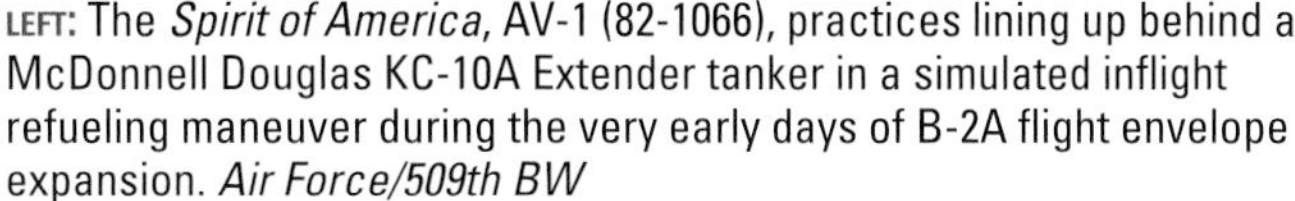

LEFT: The *Spirit of America*, AV-1 (82-1066), practices lining up behind a McDonnell Douglas KC-10A Extender tanker in a simulated inflight refueling maneuver during the very early days of B-2A flight envelope expansion. *Air Force/509th BW*

TOP RIGHT: The *Spirit of America*, AV-1 (82-1066), and the *Spirit of Arizona*, AV-2 (82-1067), line up to take on fuel from an Air Force KC-10A Extender (79-1951). *Air Force/509th BW*

BOTTOM RIGHT: Somewhere over the southern Sierra Mountains northwest of Edwards AFB, the *Spirit of New York*, AV-3 (82-1068), positions under a Boeing KC-135R Stratotanker following the refueling location lights on the belly of the tanker. Only then can the "Boom Operator" fly the boom into the B-2As inflight-refueling receptacle to begin the thirty minutes or so that the two aircraft are connected. *Air Force/509th BW*

TOP RIGHT: The *Spirit of America* takes off on July 17, 1989, from the Northrop Grumman production facility in Palmdale, CA, on its inaugural flight to Edwards Air Force Base, CA. The B-2A would remain in the testing phase until 1993, when the first operational aircraft was delivered to Whiteman AFB, MO. *Air Force/509th BW*

BOTTOM LEFT: A front-left view of the *Spirit of America*, then called the Advanced Technology Bomber, on the runway at the Air Force Flight Test Center for its first test flight. *Air Force/509th BW*

BOTTOM CENTER: A right rear view of the *Spirit of America* on the runway at the Air Force Flight Test Center for its first test flight. *Air Force/509th BW*

BOTTOM RIGHT: A front-left view of the *Spirit of America* on the runway at the Air Force Flight Test Center for its first test flight. The red diamond shapes are for in-flight photo calibration. *Air Force/509th BW*

TOP LEFT: The fifth B-2A, the *Spirit of Ohio*, AV-5 (82-1070), taxis by AV-1, the *Spirit of America*, then known as "Fatal Beauty," and was placed in flyable storage at Air Force Plant 42, Site 4, in Palmdale, CA, in March 1993 after eighty-one sorties accumulating 362.6 flight hours. The two B-2A airframes behind AV-1 are the two static airframes, AV-998 and AV-997. *Northrop Grumman*

BOTTOM LEFT: Two generations of Stealth fly in formation over Edwards AFB, CA. The Lockheed Martin F-117A, carrying an "ED" tail code, flies in close formation with the *Spirit of New York*, AV-3 (82-1068), then known as "The Ghost." *Air Force/509th BW*

RIGHT: On the ramp at Edwards South Base B-2A flight test facility, "Fatal Beauty," AV-1 (82-1066), taxis by AV-2 (82-1067), then known as "The Ship From Hell" or "Murphy's Law." Today it is called the *Spirit of Arizona*. *Northrop Grumman*

TOP LEFT: The *Spirit of New York*, AV-3 (82-1068), sports a very unusual series of stripping on both the upper and lower starboard leading edge. The lines are calibration markings used during icing testing. The B-2A would fly behind a specially modified KC-135 Stratotanker that sprayed water to test the B-2A's ability to shed the ice and still maintain control. *USAF via Tony Landis*

BOTTOM LEFT: The *Spirit of New York* flying slow with gear extended and the unique split ailerons opened about 50%, off the coast of Vandenberg AFB, CA. *Air Force/509th BW*

TOP RIGHT: The *Spirit of New York* heads down the Edwards AFB main runway in preparation for conducting additional icing tests. *USAF via Tony Landis*

BOTTOM RIGHT: A bottom view of the *Spirit of New York*'s anti-icing markings on the underside of the starboard leading edge of the B-2A. *USAF via Tony Landis*

TOP RIGHT: The *Spirit of Mississippi*, AV-6 (82-1071), flies over the Mojave Desert northeast of Edwards AFB during envelope expansion testing. Prior to the formal naming ceremony, AV-6 was called "Black Widow." AV-6 spent six months in a hangar and was taken completely apart and put back together in order to write a maintenance dock service manual, and to validate the process. *Air Force/509th BW*

BOTTOM: *Spirit of Arizona* taxis during a Nuclear Operational Readiness Exercise at Whiteman Air Force Base, MO, August 29, 2009. Eight B-2As were gathered simultaneously at a moment's notice, supporting the Whiteman mission of safely, securely and effectively providing combat-ready forces for nuclear deterrence and global strike operations. *Air Force/509th BW*

During the flight-testing of the B-2, there needed to be a way to validate the specific Radar Cross Section or RCS of the B-2A. Hughes (now Raytheon), the prime contractor for the "Low Probability of Intercept" AN/APQ-181 Radar System, decided to utilize their NTA-3B Douglas Skywarrior as a flying LO validation platform.

The NTA-3B, a.k.a. the "Whale," had the ability to look at the RCS of the B-2, in flight and conduct very precise measurements. In addition to the custom-built radar, the Whale had what is called "Skyballs." It utilized two high-definition steerable cameras under the nose radome and in the tail cone. *Mike Glenn*

The radar unit employed on the NTA-3B was custom-built and made of parts from other programs. The radar antennas were both coupled to a high-resolution radar transmitter/receiver in the aft crew area of the NTA-3B, and were selectable to be either linked to the nose or tail antenna.

During validation testing, the NTA-3B would either start at the back of the B-2A and fly around the B-2A, or in front of the B-2A and have the B-2A transition around the NTA-3B. The transition front to back, or back to front, took just sixty seconds. This fly-around window was used to look for hot points where the LO coatings had imperfections, and were in need of attention once back on the ground.

Initially, the NTA-3B was under contract to Northrop for LO validation and was used for pre-delivery of the B-2A to Air Force. In order to ensure the B-2A did in fact meet its LO requirements, the Air Force contracted the NTA-3B for their own pre-delivery testing, and all twenty-one B-2As delivered to Air Force were checked out utilizing this platform. *Mike Glenn*

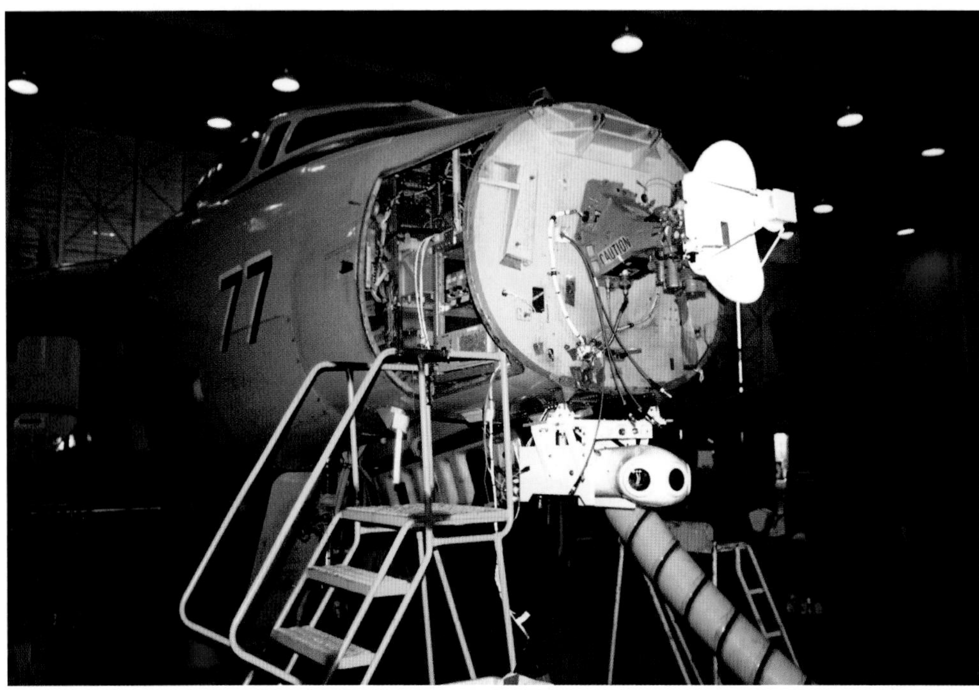

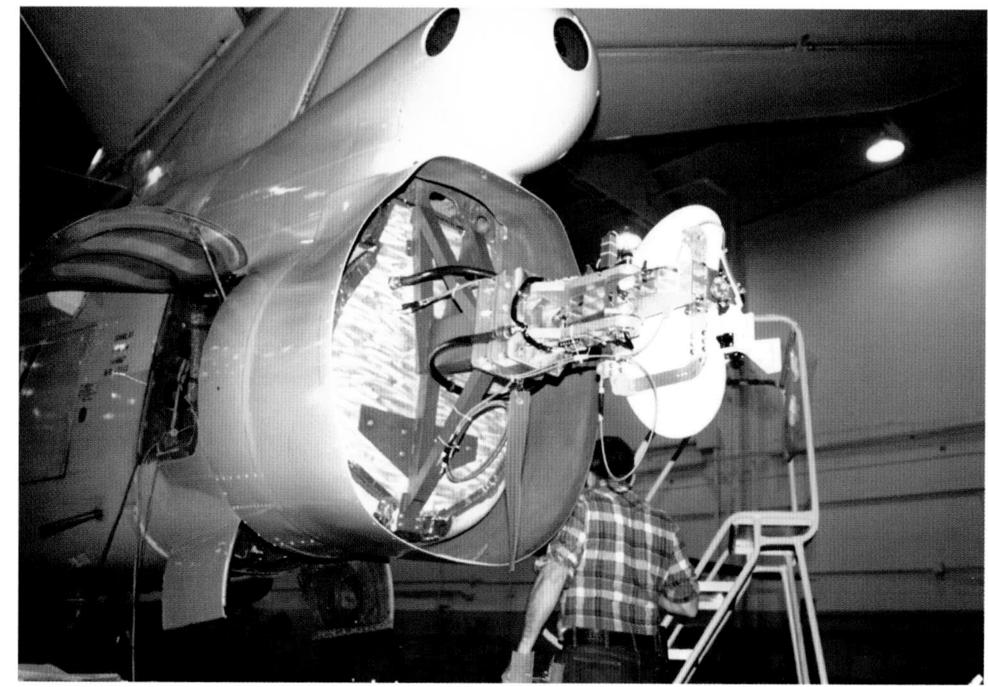

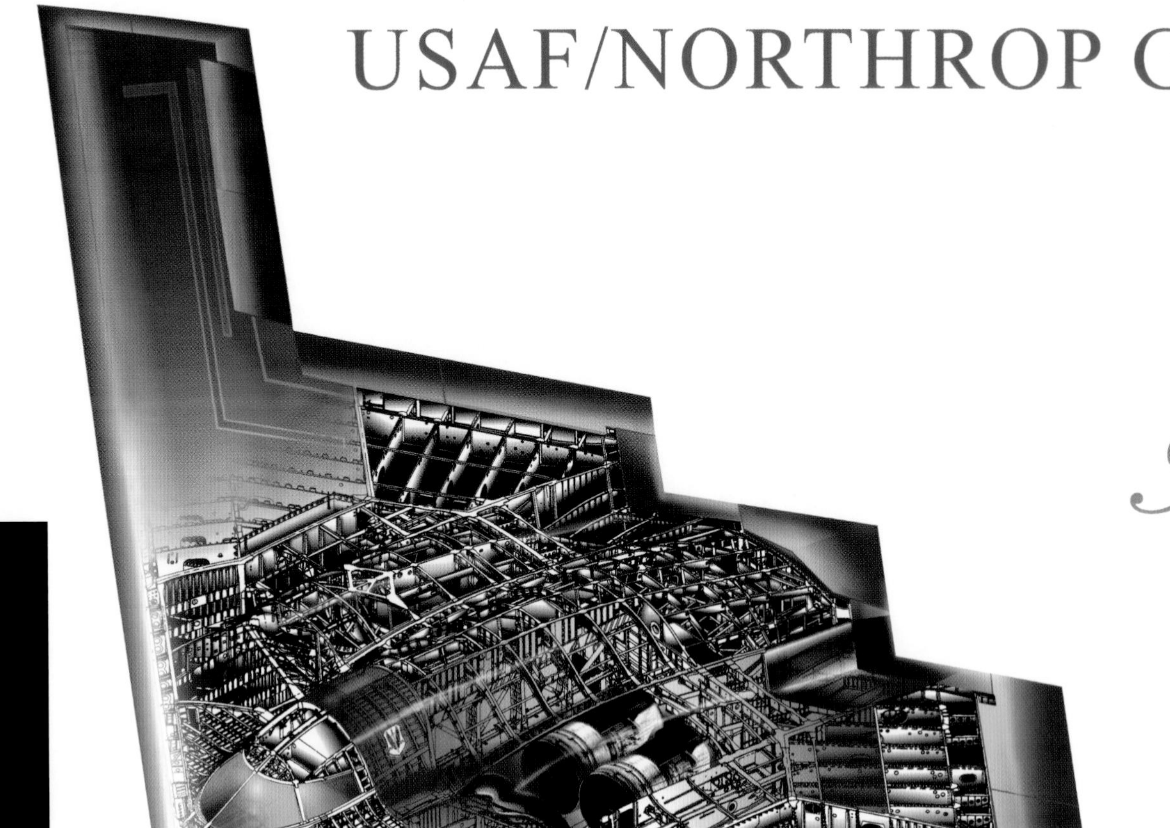

USAF/NORTHROP GRUMMAN

Spirit Is About to Go Operational

TOP LEFT: The *Spirit of New York*, AV-3 (82-1068), shown just lifting off during an airshow at Edwards AFB, CA and still carrying the Edwards "ED" code on the main gear doors. *Author's collection*

TOP CENTER: Bottom view of the *Spirit of New York* as it does a flyby over the Edwards airshow flight line. *Author's collection*

TOP RIGHT: The *Spirit of New York* banks over the Edwards AFB, CA, airshow attendees during its flight demonstration. *Author's collection*

BOTTOM LEFT: The *Spirit of New York,* on a landing approach at Whiteman AFB, MO, was the first B-2A with a complete avionics suite, and was utilized for radar, navigation, offensive and defensive systems testing. AV-3 was named the *Spirit of New York* on October 10, 1997, and was upgraded to full Block 30 specifications by 2002. *Air Force/509th BW*

TOP LEFT: The *Spirit of Missouri*, AV-8 (88-0329), was the first B-2A delivered to the 509th Bomb Wing on December 17, 1993, and was named on the same day. This B-2A is the one that was flown to the Paris Air Show on June 11–12, 1995. It was upgraded to Block 30 standards in November 1997. *Air Force/509th BW*

MIDDLE LEFT: The *Spirit of Missouri* as it arrives at Andersen AFB, Guam. *Air Force/509th BW*

BOTTOM LEFT: The *Spirit of Missouri* on the ramp at Andersen AFB, Guam, on October 11, 1998. *Air Force/509th BW*

BOTTOM RIGHT: A night shot of the *Spirit of Missouri* on the flight line at Whiteman AFB, MO. *Air Force/509th BW*

The *Spirit of America*, AV-1 (82-1066), on the taxiway at Whiteman AFB, MO. AV-1 was modified to Block 30 standards and delivered to Whiteman on July 14, 2000. *Don Logan*

TOP: Col. Andrew Gebara, 509th Bomb Wing vice commander, stands in front the B-2A *Spirit of Nebraska*, AV-13 (89-0128), on July 29, 2011. This is Gebara's third time stationed at Whiteman throughout his twenty-year career. *Air Force/509th BW*

BOTTOM: Royal Air Force Flight Lieutenant Ian Hart, GR4 Tornado pilot, stands in front of the *Spirit of Louisiana*, AV-21 (93-1088), at RAF Fairford, England, on June 10, 2014. Hart is part of a United States-United Kingdom exchange program, where he trains alongside American B-2A pilots. Since 2012, he has been flying the B-2A as part of the 13th Bomb Squadron, Whiteman Air Force Base, MO. *Air Force/509th BW*

LEFT: Maj. Kristin Goodwin and Capt. Jenn Jeffords review checklists before a B-2A Spirit bomber mission on October 18, 2013. Flying the *Spirit of Mississippi*, AV-6 (82-1071), the first all-female flight crew practiced conventional bombing and refueled with a KC-135 Stratotanker from Altus Air Force Base, OK. The two cockpit crewmembers are assigned to the 325th Bomb Squadron here. Maj. Goodwin has been a B-2A pilot since May 2002 and Capt. Jeffords became B-2-certified in August 2013. *Air Force/509th BW*

RIGHT: Standing in front of the *Spirit of Alaska*, AV-15 (90-0040), on April 23, 2013, Cptns. Jennie Swiechowicz and Nicola Polidor, both 393rd Bomb Squadron B-2A Spirit pilots, are part of an elite group at Whiteman Air Force Base, MO. Sweichowicz and Polidor both dreamed of flying while growing up. *Air Force/509th BW*

An Inside Look at the Spirit

TOP LEFT: Two B-2A Spirits from the 509th Bomb Wing, the *Spirit of Oklahoma*, AV-18 (93-1085), and the *Spirit of Alaska*, AV-15 (90-0040), in a nighttime photo at RAF Fairford after a nine-hour flight from Whiteman AFB, MO. This was the first time that two of these aircraft stood on British soil at the same time. *Tony Osborne*

BOTTOM LEFT: Staff Sgt. Eric Barnes, 509th Maintenance Squadron test cell assistant section chief, and Airman 1st Class Lester Popham, 509th MXS aerospace propulsion apprentice, close an inlet bell mouth for a B-2A Spirit engine inside the test cell, February 13, 2013. The inlet bell mouth distributes and guides air into the motor to allow the engine to run smoothly in the test cell. *Air Force/509th BW*

BOTTOM CENTER: AEDC Test Operations personnel make final inspections of an F118-GE-100 engine prior to altitude testing. The engine, which powers the B-2A bomber, is part of the F118 Service Life Extension Program. *AEDC*

LEFT: Airman 1st Class Lester Popham, 509th Maintenance Squadron aerospace propulsion apprentice, inspects the exhaust of a B-2A Spirit engine for foreign object debris and oil in the test cell, February 13, 2013. A thorough inspection helps mechanics find items that might destroy the engine or the test cell. *Air Force/509th BW*

RIGHT: Senior Airman Kaitlyn Fawber, 509th Maintenance Squadron aerospace propulsion journeyman, shines a flashlight on a test cell exhaust tube rivet, February 13, 2013. The rivet maintains the sound proofing in the cell. *Air Force/509th BW*

B-2 Spirit Egress Trainer and Survival Equipment

The evolution of the 509th Bomb Wing "Egress Trainer" had a very interesting journey starting as an "Ejection seat test fixture," only to be sold for scrap in the late 1990s to a Jesse Lazano of Little Rock, CA.

Once the B-2A was operational, they needed a fixture to train a B-2A crew on the safest and fastest way to exit the B-2A in the event of a crash landing. The Air Force approached Mr. Lazano asking to buy the "Ejection seat test fixture" back for what he paid for it. He said no and more than tripled the price to the Air Force to buy it back. *James C. Goodall*

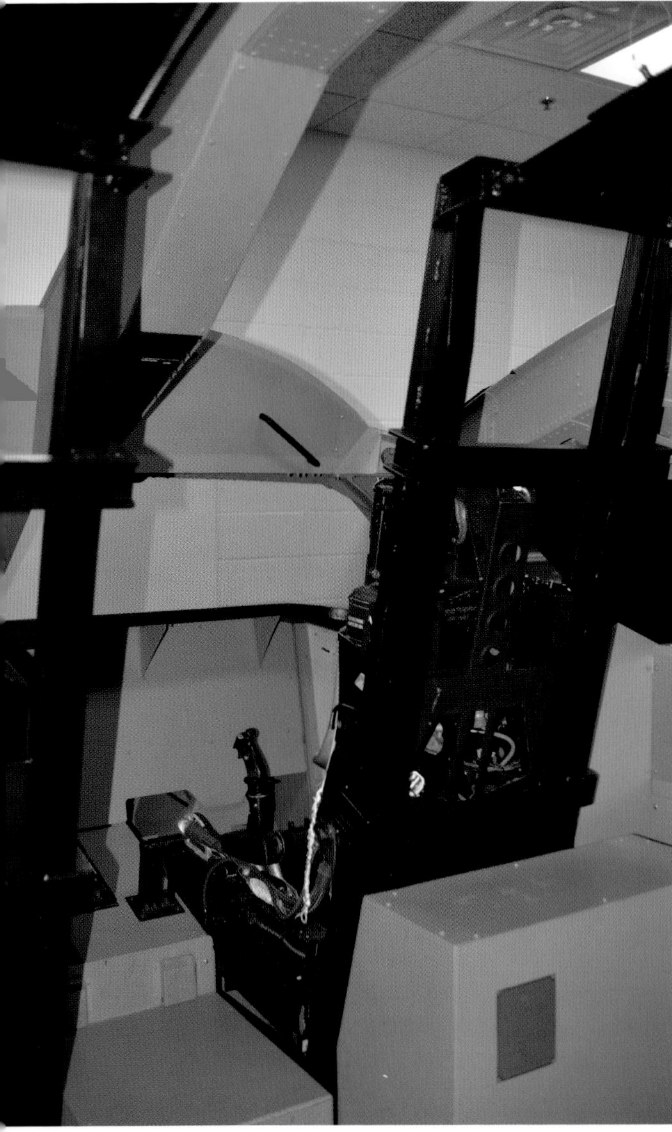

TOP LEFT: The inside of the "Egress Trainer" is sparse and is only functional as a means to train pilots to get out fast and safe. *James C. Goodall*

TOP RIGHT: An additional trainer, with a video link simulating what is happening outside the aircraft, goes through proper procedures for leaving the airplane. *James C. Goodall*

BOTTOM RIGHT: Illustrations from an unclassified B-2A handbook. *Author's collection*

ESCAPE HATCHES

SEAT EQUIPMENT COMPONENT LOCATION

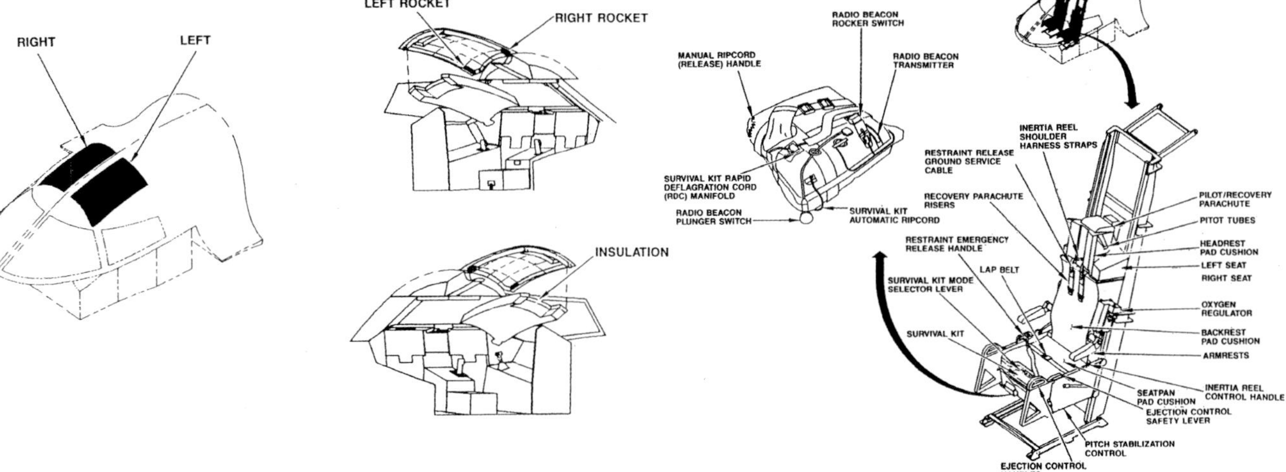

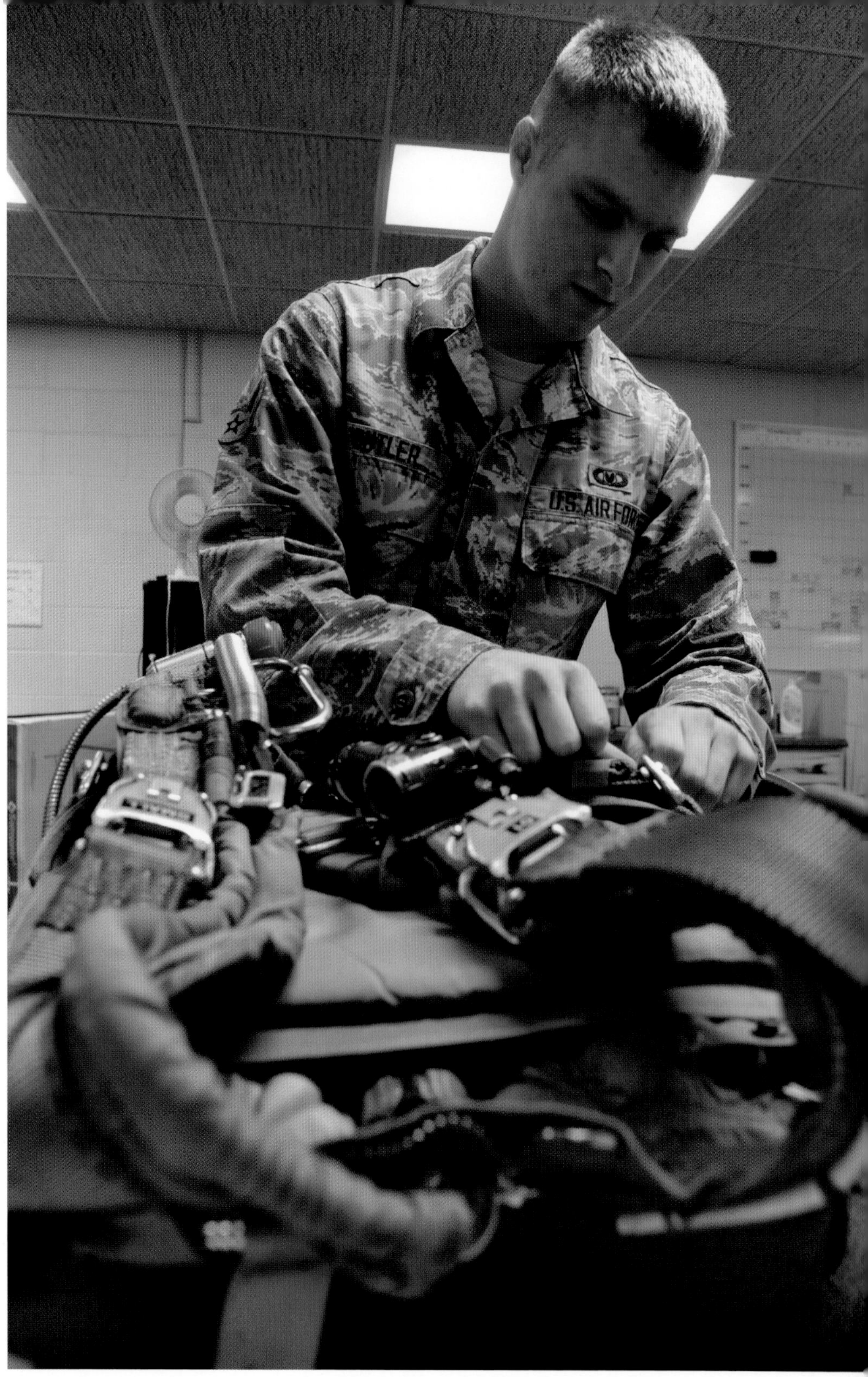

LEFT: Taking inspiration from "Storm Troopers" in the various *Star Wars* movies, the Air Force developed a nuclear face shield that would protect the crew's eyes in the event a nuclear weapon was deployed. The glass is totally transparent up to the point of a detonation where in a few nanoseconds the glass turns opaque, preventing permanent damage to the crew's vision. *James C. Goodall*

RIGHT: Airman 1st Class William Butler, 509th Operations Support Squadron aircrew flight equipment technician, inspects the pockets of a parachute to ensure the presence of strobe lights, Whiteman Air Force Base, MO, October 9, 2013. Strobe lights are used to signal rescue once the pilot has ejected and is awaiting extraction. *Air Force/509th BW*

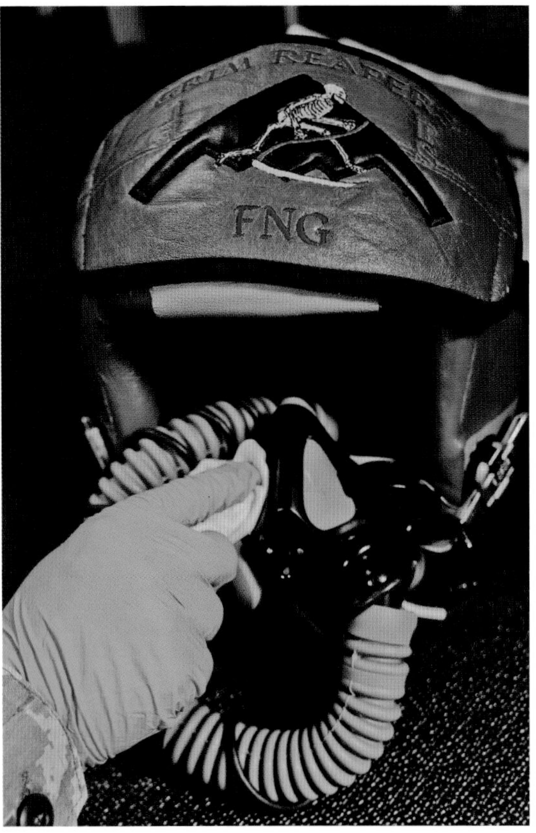

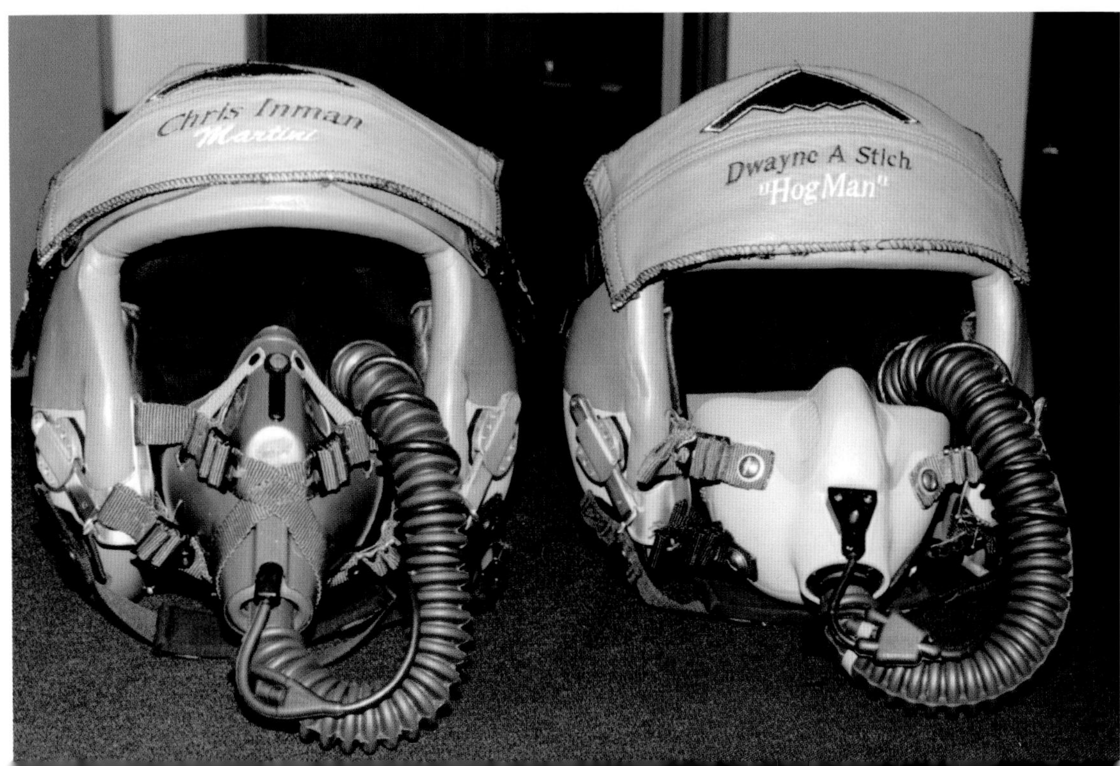

TOP LEFT: In the Life Support section, when not in use, all of the crews' equipment is stored, maintained, and serviced to ensure proper fit and functionality. *James C. Goodall*

TOP CENTER: Even in the Air Force there is certain amount of humor that creeps in now and then. This particular helmet, for one of the new pilots of the Missouri Air National Guard's 131st Bomb Wing of the 13th Bomb Squadron, sports a face shield cover with the "Grim Reapers" logo and, in place of a pilot's name, the initials "FNG," which stands for "F'ing New Guy." *Air Force/509th BW*

BOTTOM LEFT: Various oxygen masks used by B-2A crewmembers. *James C. Goodall*

TOP RIGHT: A new directive has been issued to the media not to publish the names or handles of current operational B-2A Spirit crews with their photos. Here, a B-2A crew waits for the crew van to take them to their aircraft. *James C. Goodall*

TOP LEFT: The Whiteman AFB tower and a view of the expansive ramp needed to handle a large aircraft such as the B-2A Spirit. *James C. Goodall*

BOTTOM LEFT: SSgt Joshua Batman, 509th Operations Support Squadron air traffic controller, operates a light gun at Whiteman Air Force Base, MO, July 10, 2014. The light gun is used to communicate safety and movement signals to individuals on the flight line. *Air Force/509th BW*

BOTTOM CENTER-LEFT: Staff duty officer, a captain (name removed for security reasons) checks in with the command post for a current update of B-2A and other aircraft movements. *James C. Goodall*

BOTTOM CENTER-RIGHT: Airman 1st Class Chanel Johnson, 509th Operations Support Squadron air traffic control apprentice, writes on a flight progress strip at Whiteman Air Force Base, MO, July 10, 2014. Flight progress strips are used to keep track of aircraft missions, and contain the aircraft name, type, departure time, and instructions for landing. *Air Force/509th BW*

BOTTOM RIGHT: Senior Airman Craig Gephardt, 509th Operations Support Squadron air traffic controller, operates the flight data systems in the tower at Whiteman Air Force Base, MO, July 10, 2014. The flight data systems contain flight plans for every aircraft operating within the Kansas City Center airspace. *Air Force/509th BW*

The Beast in Detail

TOP LEFT: From the very beginning, B-2s have had a major on-going maintenance problem with external exhaust surface cracking, which is related to its low observable design, and the coefficient of expansion of the various pieces and parts that made up the external exhaust structure. To correct this maintenance headache, the new exhaust ramp is a woven metal shield that can expand and contract without cracking. *Northrop Grumman*

TOP CENTER: This photo was taken in the early days of the B-2 buildup and shows AV-1 (82-1066), now called *Spirit of America,* with its leading edges removed, clearly showing the leading edge structure. The B-2A closest to the camera is AV-2 (82-1067), *Spirit of Arizona,* with its "Beaver Tail" removed and a look down the starboard exhaust tailpipe. It is also possible to see the trailing edge structure partially hidden behind the clear vinyl sheeting. *Northrop Grumman*

TOP RIGHT: Maintenance personnel from the 509th Bomb Wing's maintenance squadron replace shuttle-like head shedding tiles on the upper surface of the exhaust ejector. The exhaust area of the B-2 has always been a maintenance problem; hopefully, the new style woven ramp will reduce the number of man hours in this area. *Northrop Grumman*

CENTER: Northrop developed a one-piece tail pipe exhaust ejector for use on the B-2A Spirit. *Northrop Grumman*

BOTTOM LEFT: A cutaway of the inboard engine nacelle showing the location of the engine, exhaust pipe, and related antenna and sub systems. *Jim Goodall Drawing*

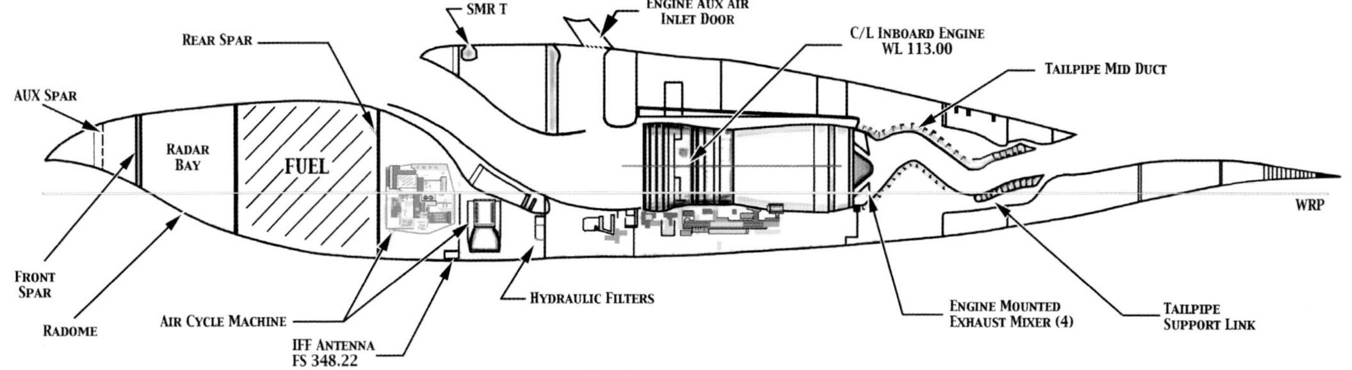

AN/APQ-181 Radar System

TOP LEFT: Illustration from an unclassified B-2A handbook. *Author's collection*

TOP RIGHT: A poor quality image, but the only one ever published, of the Hughes/Raytheon AN/APQ-181 "Low-Probability-of-Intercept" radar. *Author's collection*

BOTTOM: B-2 crew performing a preflight check of the *Spirit of Missouri*, AV-8 (88-0329), in one of twelve dedicated hangars used to protect each of the base's B-2As. *James C. Goodall*

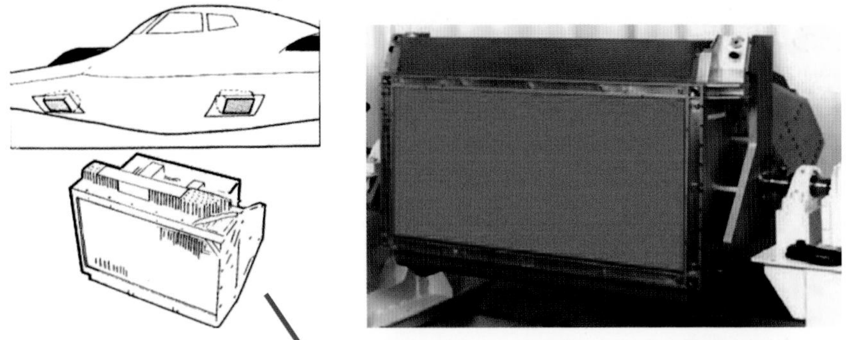

REFUELING LIGHTS

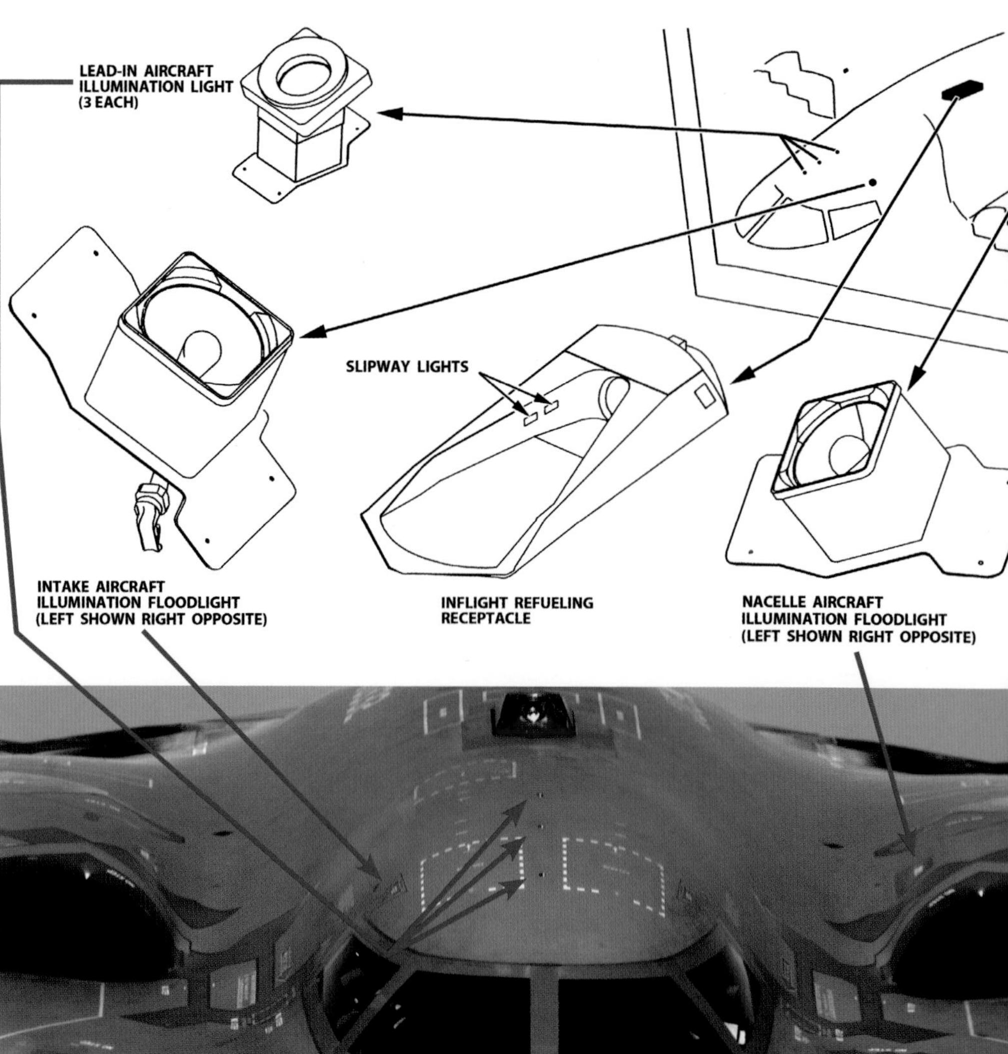

Refueling Lights

TOP: Illustration from an unclassified B-2A handbook. *Author's collection*

BOTTOM: *Air Force/509th BW*

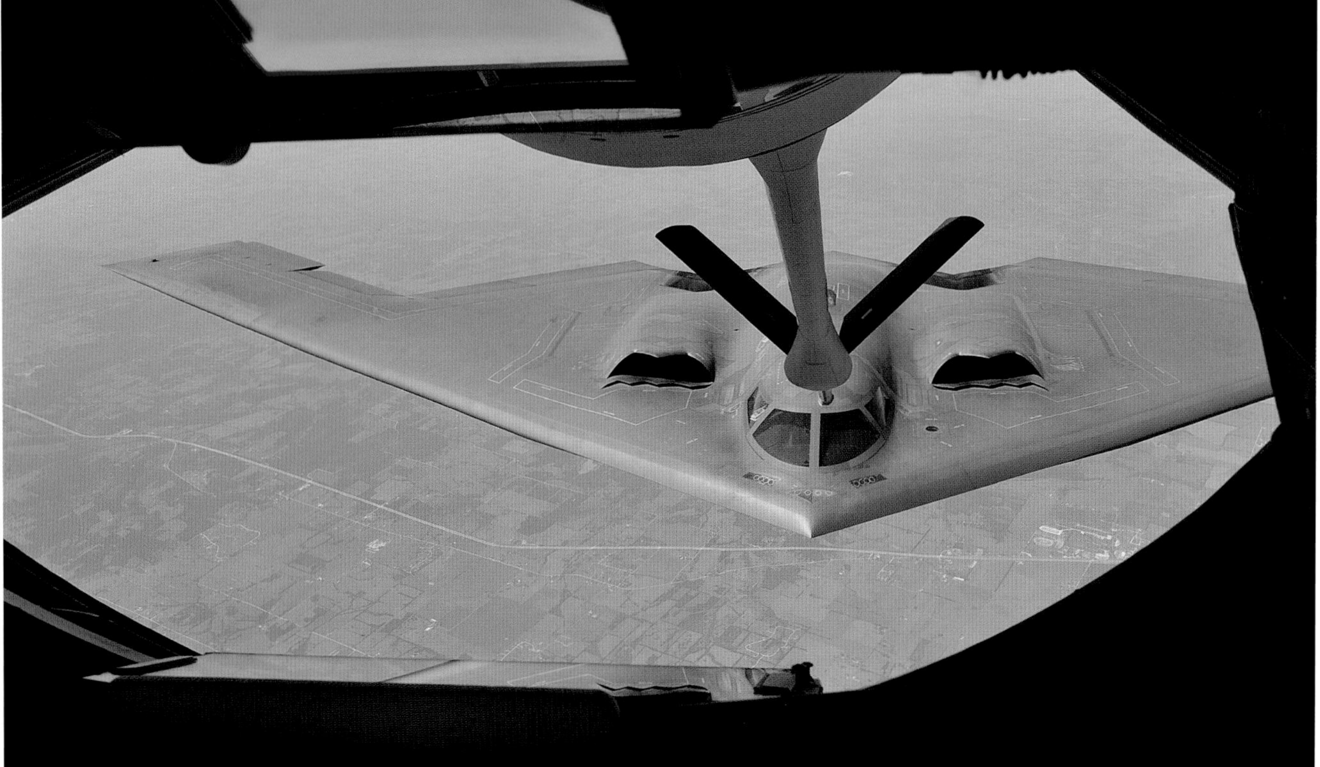

TOP LEFT: One of the more dramatic views of a B-2A the *Spirit of Nebraska*, AV-13 (89-0128), from the "Boom Operators" position over a cloud-covered countryside somewhere over Kansas. *Air Force/509th BW*

BOTTOM LEFT: *Spirit of Nebraska* prepares to receive fuel from a KC-135 Stratotanker during a mission in the European theater supporting NATO Operation Allied Force. *Air Force/509th BW*

TOP RIGHT: *Spirit of Nebraska* takes on fuel from a KC-135R assigned to the 452nd Air Mobility Wing, March Air Force Reserve Base, Riverside, CA. *Air Force/509th BW*

ASTROINERTIAL INSTRUMENT

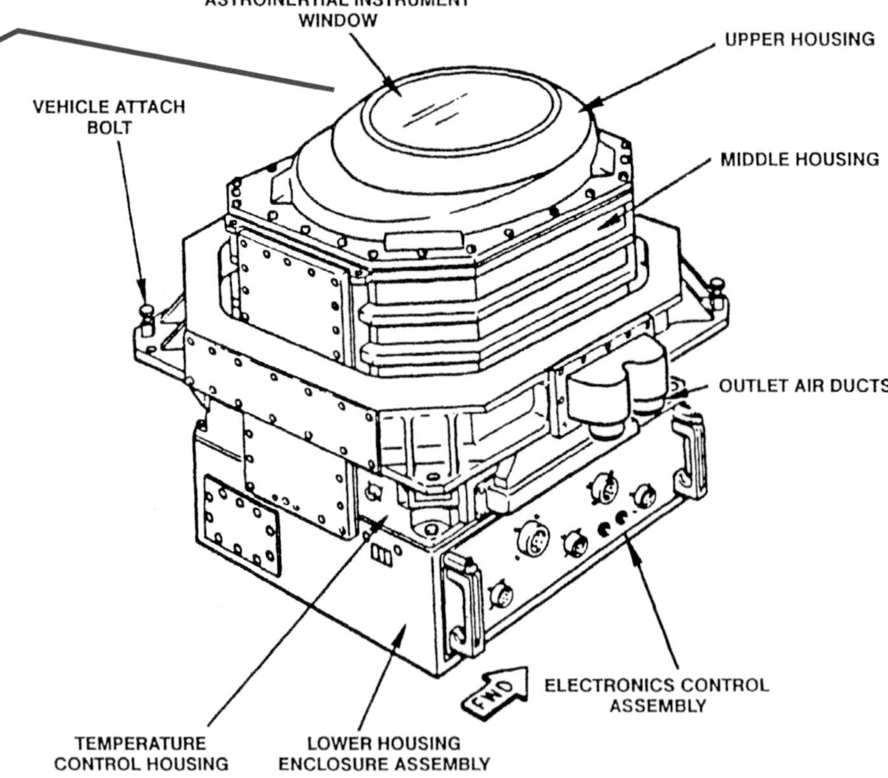

WHAT IS ASTROINERTIAL?

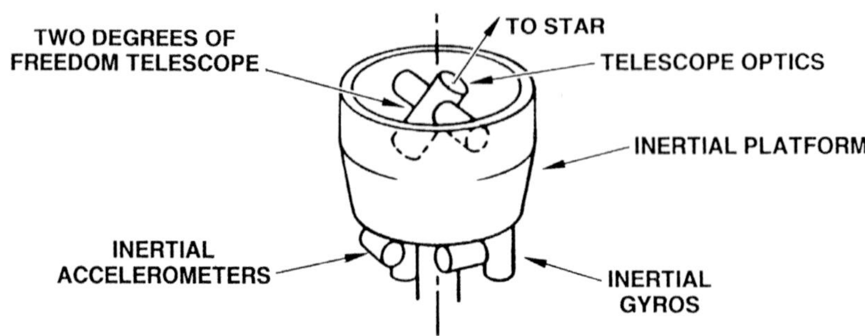

- INERTIAL PLATFORM PROVIDES VERTICAL PLUS INSTANTANEOUS NAV DATA (VELOCITY, HEADING, POSITION)
- STAR TRACKER PROVIDES
  — POSITION UPDATES
  — ACCURATE HEADING
  — CALIBRATION OF GYRO DRIFT RATES FOR NEAR-PERFECT GYRO PERFORMANCE
- WORLDWIDE AND DAY/NIGHT TRACKING
  — CONSISTENTLY TRACKS DOWN TO SEA LEVEL IN FULL DAYLIGHT (CLEAR SKY)

Astroinertial Instrument

LEFT: A topside view of the *Spirit of Alaska*, AV-15 (90-0040), showing the position of the Astroinertial Instrument, or "Astro Tracker," in its hangar at Whiteman AFB, MO. This unit is very similar to that used on the Lockheed SR-71 and can track up to twelve star formations on the ground and in broad daylight. *James C. Goodall*

RIGHT: Illustration from an unclassified B-2A handbook showing the Astor Tracker with descriptions of the various components of the system. *Author's collection*

Boeing Developed Advanced Rotary Launcher

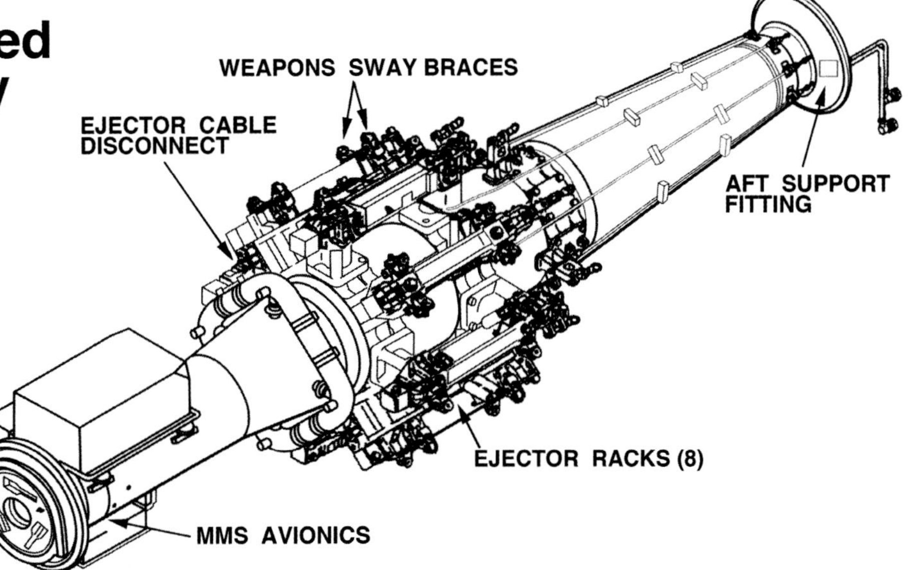

Boeing Built and Designed Advance Rotary Launcher

TOP: Illustration from an unclassified B-2A handbook showing the major components of the Boeing-built Advanced Rotary Launcher. *Author's collection*

BOTTOM LEFT: Inside the B-2A's weapons bay looking forward, showing the major components of the Boeing-built Advanced Rotary Launcher. *James C. Goodall*

BOTTOM CENTER: The last Boeing-built and designed Advanced Rotary Launcher for the B-2A Spirit being prepped for shipment to Whitman AFB, MO, from the Boeing military facility located on the west side of Boeing Field, just a few miles south of downtown Seattle. *Boeing*

BOTTOM RIGHT: Inside the B-2A's weapons bay looking aft showing the major components of the Boeing built Advanced Rotary Launcher. *James C. Goodall*

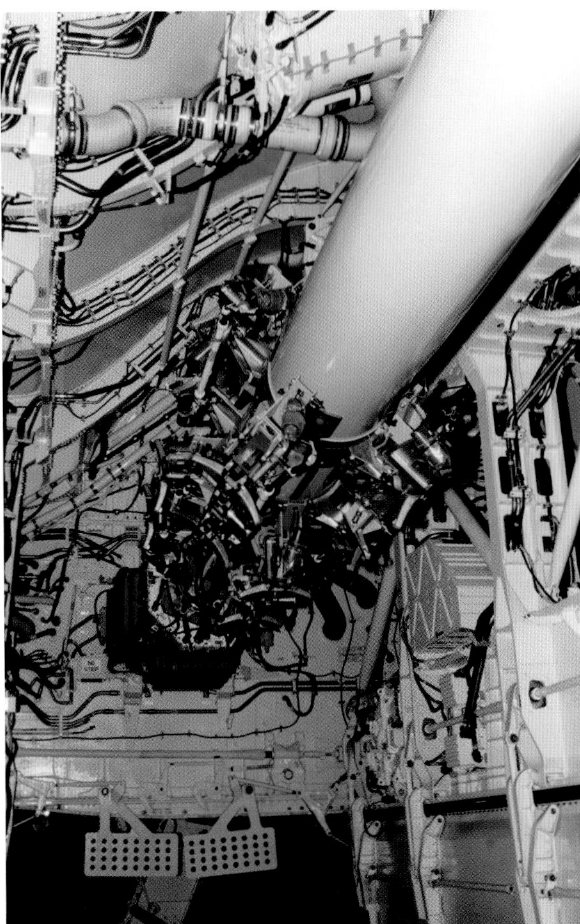

LEFT: Weapons specialist, TSgt Connors and a 393rd Weapons Load Crew member works with a Boeing technician on the proper maintenance of the Boeing developed Advanced Rotary Launcher. *Air Force/509th BW*

TOP RIGHT: 393rd Weapons Load Crew Chief, SSgt Chip Littrel, and 393rd Weapons Load Crew member, SSgt Robert Vonada, load weapons onto the B-2A Bomber for the Turkey Shoot competition held on August 15, 2002; the Turkey Shoot is a wing bombing competition held twice a year. Both the 393rd and 325th Bomb Squadrons competed in the August 2002 competition. *Air Force/509th BW*

BOTTOM RIGHT: Weapons Specialist, SSgt Andrew Chocha adjusts the connection points on a rotary launcher assembly on the B-2A Spirit Bomber, the *Spirit of America*, AV-1 (82-166), prior to its departure at Whiteman Air Force Base on March 20, 2003, in support of Operation Iraqi Freedom. *Air Force/509th BW*

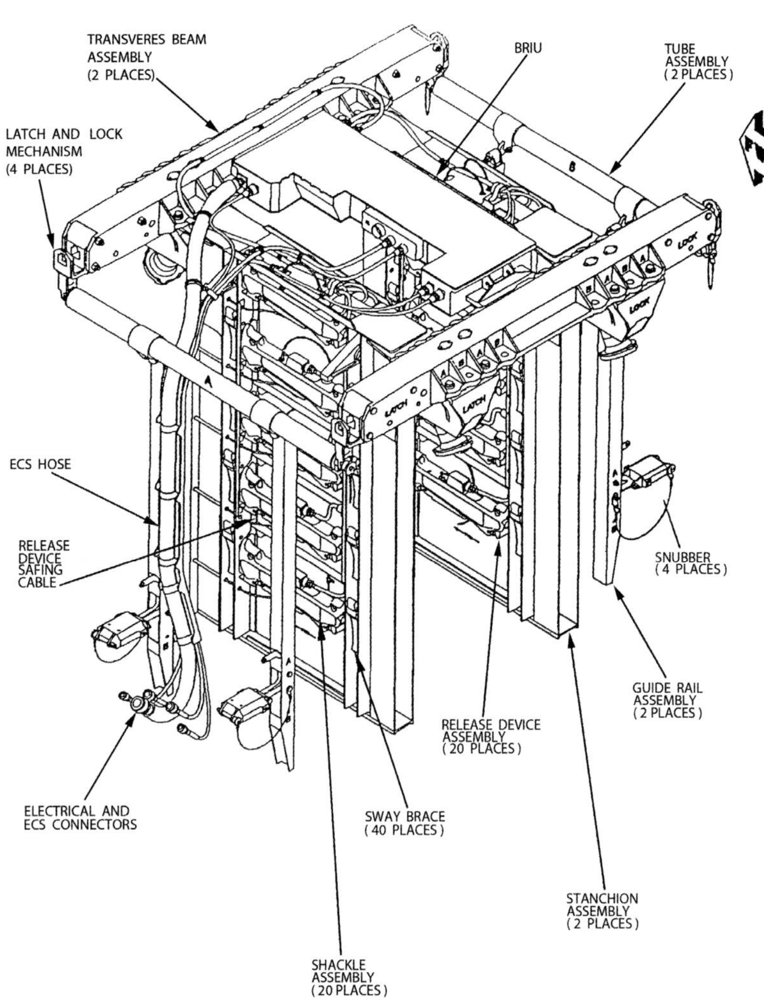

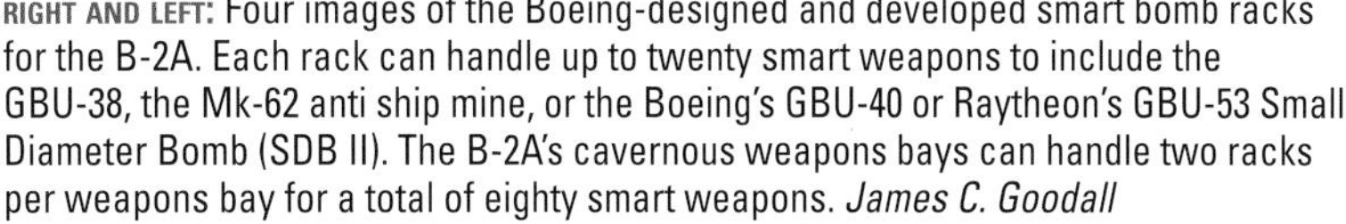

RIGHT AND LEFT: Four images of the Boeing-designed and developed smart bomb racks for the B-2A. Each rack can handle up to twenty smart weapons to include the GBU-38, the Mk-62 anti ship mine, or the Boeing's GBU-40 or Raytheon's GBU-53 Small Diameter Bomb (SDB II). The B-2A's cavernous weapons bays can handle two racks per weapons bay for a total of eighty smart weapons. *James C. Goodall*

TOP CENTER: An illustration from an unclassified B-2A handbook showing the Boeing-developed smart bomb rack assembly. *Author's collection*

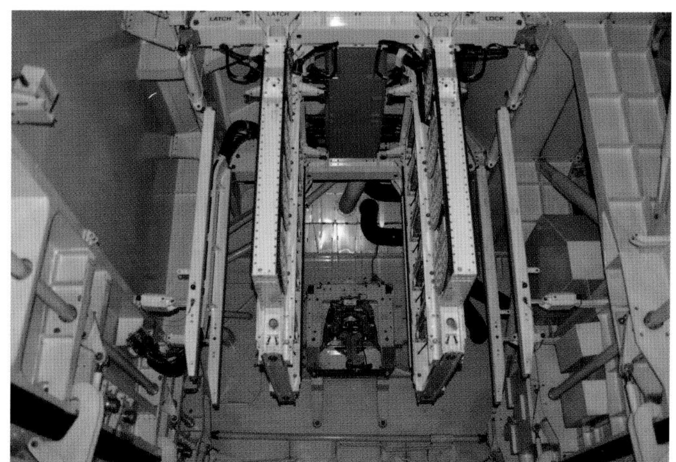

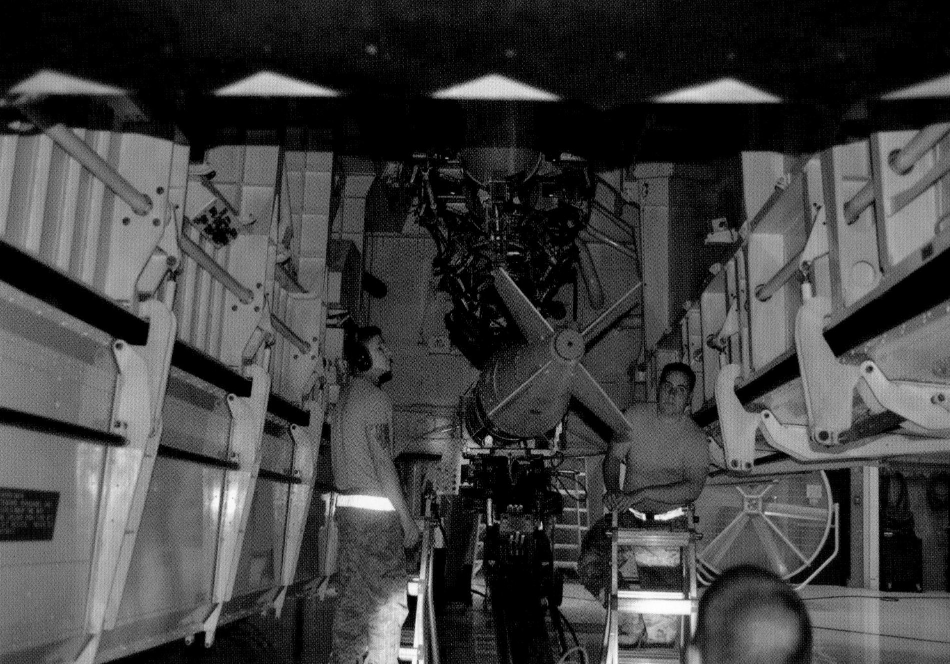

TOP LEFT: The MHU-83 D/E "Jammer" is a self-propelled munitions handling unit with a diesel-driven hydrostatic system also supplying the lift boom functions of lift, yaw, tilt to facilitate to loading of weapons into the weapons bay of the B-2A Spirit. *James C. Goodall*

BOTTOM, LEFT: Two airmen from the 393rd Weapons Squadron prepare to load a 2,000-pound BLU-109 penetrating bomb into the B-2A Weapons Trainer on June 3, 2014. *James C. Goodall*

TOP RIGHT: A 393rd Weapons Squadron technician gently inches the MHU-83 "Jammer" beneath the 2,000-pound BLU-109. The cradle on the MHU-83 allows for rotation of the weapon through the "X", "Y," and "Z" axis to allow for quick and safe loading. *James C. Goodall*

BOTTOM RIGHT: The legs of the MHU-83 extent outward when needed to ensure the platform is stable during the movement of the weapon. It has a lift capability of 7,000 pounds. *James C. Goodall*

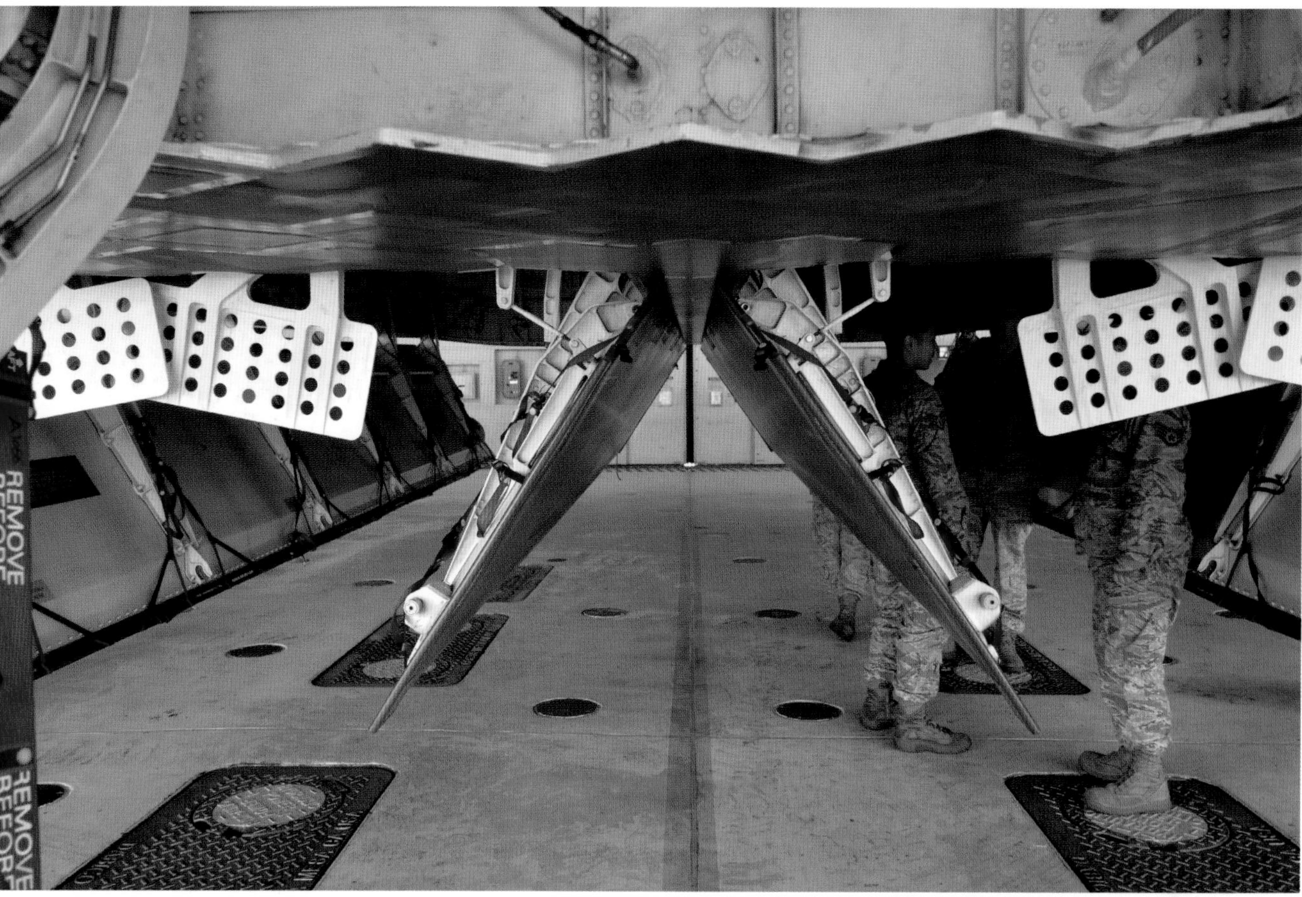

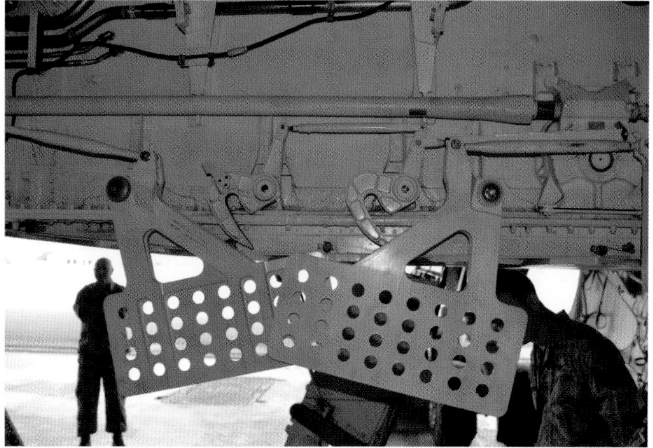

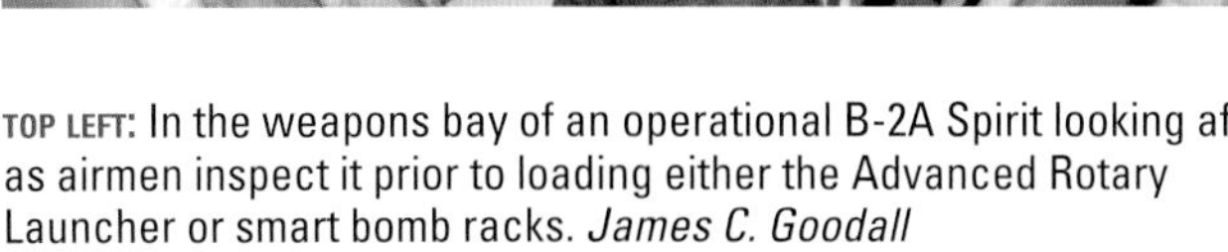

TOP LEFT: In the weapons bay of an operational B-2A Spirit looking aft as airmen inspect it prior to loading either the Advanced Rotary Launcher or smart bomb racks. *James C. Goodall*

TOP RIGHT: Detail view of the wind deflectors on the forward leading edge of the B-2As massive weapons bays. In this view, the bomb bay doors are only opened part way. When dropping eighty GPS guided weapons, these doors are only opened for about two to four seconds each. *James C. Goodall*

BOTTOM CENTER: A close-up view of the B-2A Spirit's weapons bay wind deflectors. If the deflectors were not installed, severe turbulence could cause the weapons' release to be chaotic, affecting the safe and reliable release of the bomber's weapons. *James C. Goodall*

BOTTOM RIGHT: A forward-looking view in the B-2A's weapons bay. The circular object in the center of the bay is the attachment for the Boeing Advanced Rotary Launcher with all of its associated connections and umbilical hookups. *James C. Goodall*

TOP LEFT: From left to right: A1C Tommy Day, SrA Phillip Ruiz, and TSgt Dwayne Bolles, all weapons specialists from the 509th Aircraft Maintenance Squadron, Whiteman AFB, MO, prepare to load a BDU-56 bomb on a B-2A, the *Spirit of Pennsylvania*, AV-20 (93-1085), from the 509th Bomb Wing also based at Whiteman AFB, during their deployment at Andersen AFB, Guam, on April 11, 2005. *Air Force/509th BW*

BOTTOM LEFT: SSgt Michael Taylor (left) and SrA Joseph Nelson load a bomb onto a B-2A Spirit. They are weapons specialists deployed from the 509th Aircraft Maintenance Squadron at Whiteman AFB, MO. *Air Force/509th BW*

BOTTOM CENTER: Looking under the *Spirit of Kitty Hawk*, AV-19 (93-1086), shows a bit more detail on the weapons bay door and the protective covering used on all edge surfaces on the B-2A Spirit. The edges are very critical to the overall success of the B-2As LO characteristics. *James C. Goodall*

BOTTOM RIGHT: SrA Phillip Ruiz moves a bomb to be loaded onto a B-2A Spirit. He is a weapon specialist deployed to Anderson AFB, Guam, from the 509th Aircraft Maintenance Squadron at Whiteman AFB, MO. *Air Force/509th BW*

TOP LEFT: Two 393rd Weapons Squadron technicians carefully inspect the first three of eight 2,000-pound GBU-31 (V) 1/B JDAMs attached to the Advanced Rotary Launcher. *Air Force/509th BW*

BOTTOM LEFT: A weapons NCO checks over a bomb load in support of Operation Iraqi Freedom in preparation of loading the weapons into the *Spirit of Mississippi*, AV-6, in the background. *Air Force/509th BW*

BOTTOM CENTER: A weapons load crewmember drives a weapon to be loaded onto the B-2A during the Turkey Shoot competition held on August 15, 2002, between the 393rd and the 325th Bomb Squadrons. *Air Force/509th BW*

BOTTOM RIGHT: SrA Siu Yu Leung loads an inert GBU 28-C/B bomb onto a B-2A Spirit during the annual "load crew of the year" competition on February 3, 2012. The competition is timed and judged on several aspects to include zero deficiencies during the weapons load evaluation. Leung is a weapons technician assigned to the 509th Aircraft Maintenance Squadron. *Air Force/509th BW*

TOP LEFT: Ready to go to war, the *Spirit of Mississippi*, AV-6 (82-1071), is in the process of taking on a full complement of precision-guided weapons in its massive weapons bays. *Air Force/509th BW*

BOTTOM LEFT: By comparison, when loading the Small Diameter Bomb (SDB), or the smaller 500-pound JDAMs, the weapons loading crew uses a forty-inch extension to the front end of the MHU-83 weapons loader to position the weapons in the tight fitting smart bomb racks. *James C. Goodall*

TOP RIGHT: A1C Rodney Lucas, a precision guided maintenance crewmember, attaches a cable to a Joint Direct Attack Munitions (JDAM) for testing after assembly. Internal tests ensure the tail kit on the weapon is serviceable. *Air Force/509th BW*

BOTTOM RIGHT: A weapons NCO checks over bomb load in support of Operation Iraqi Freedom in preparation of loading the weapons into the *Spirit of Mississippi*. Each B-2A can carry up to sixteen 2,000-pound JDAMs, or up to eighty 500-pound JDAMs or Small Diameter Bombs. *Air Force/509th BW*

TOP LEFT: An Air Force weapons loader from the 509th Bomb Wing preps a 2,000-pound bomb for loading into a B-2A Spirit bomber during Operation Enduring Freedom. *Air Force/509th BW*

TOP CENTER: A bomb load crewmember from the 509th Bomb Wing maneuvers an MHU-83 C/E Munitions Loader with a 2,000-pound Joint Direct Attack Munitions (JDAM) based on a Mk-84 bomb to be loaded on a B-2A Spirit during Operation Enduring Freedom. *Air Force/509th BW*

BOTTOM LEFT: TSgt Tony "Chili Dawg" Rodriguez mans the MHU-83C/E Munitions Loading System to maneuver a Joint Direct Attack Munitions (JDAM) GBU-32 2,000-pound bomb. USAF SSgt Colby Davis signals and guides the munition onto its cradle on the MHU-110 Munitions Handling Trailer during day two of Operation Iraqi Freedom. In the background sits a USAF B-2A Spirit. *Air Force/509th BW*

TOP RIGHT: An Air Force load crew from the 509th Bomb Wing prepare GBU-32, a 2,000-pound Joint Direct Attack Munitions (JDAM) to be loaded on a B-2A Spirit bomber during Operation Enduring Freedom. *Air Force/509th BW*

TOP LEFT: A1C Anthony Mejia pushes a Joint Direct Attack Munitions (JDAM) over next to another on March 25, 2003. The JDAM is being loaded into the bomb bay of a B-2A Spirit that will fly a combat sortie in support of Operation Iraqi Freedom. *Air Force/509th BW*

BOTTOM LEFT: A1C Mejia (center, kneeling) motions in A1C Corie Hudson (right) as he drives a bomb jammer loaded with a Joint Direct Attack Munitions (JDAM) on March 25, 2003. The JDAM is being loaded into the bomb bay of a B-2A Spirit, which will fly a combat sortie in support of Operation Iraqi Freedom. *Air Force/509th BW*

TOP RIGHT: Boeing and the US Air Force successfully completed their first eighty-guided weapon flight test demonstration of the Mk-82 500-pound Joint Direct Attack Munitions (JDAM). The drop took place from B-2A *Spirit of Texas,* AV-7 (88-0328), on September 10, 2003, at the Utah Test and Training Range, Hill AFB, UT.

Spirit of Texas, based at Edwards AFB, CA., flew to the Utah Test and Training Range and released the eighty GPS guided weapons in a single twenty-two-second pass. The weapons were released from four Boeing-designed and built smart bomb racks, flew their planned flight paths, and attacked all eighty targets.

"Placing maximum steel on the target is what we get paid to do as Air Force bomber pilots and that happened today in a big way," said Maj. William Power, 419th Flight Test Squadron B-2A project pilot. "Dropping eighty JDAM Mk-82s in less than thirty seconds, with each attacking their own individual targets, is truly revolutionary." *Air Force/509th BW*

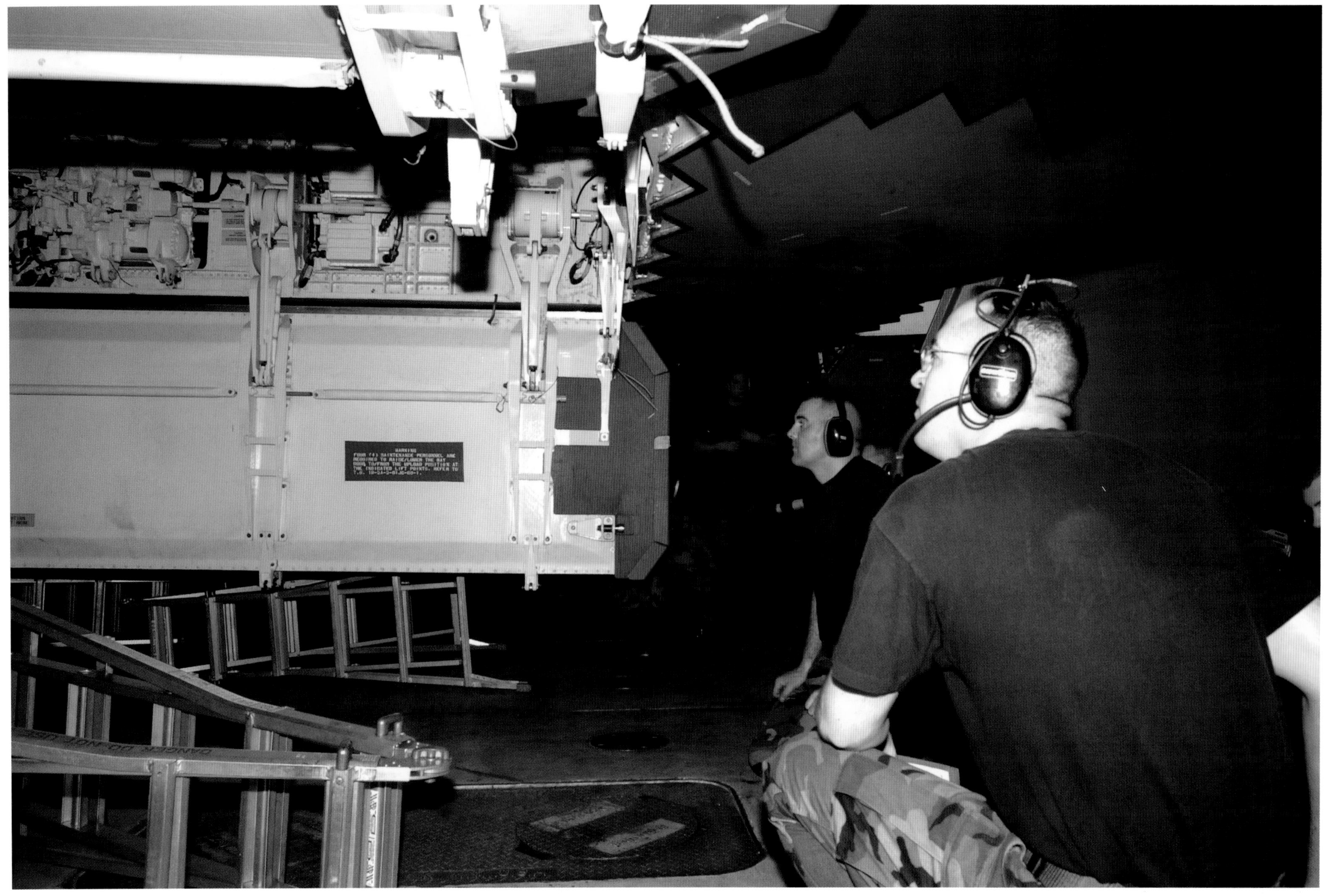

Weapons Team Member, SSgt Robert Hall (forward), and Weapons Team Chief, SSgt Michael Copeland (background), wait for a bomb jammer to place a Joint Direct Attack Munitions (JDAM) into a bomb bay of a B-2A Spirit on March 22, 2003. *Air Force/509th BW*

TOP LEFT: SrA Nicolas Cox, a weapon specialist assigned to the 509th Aircraft Maintenance Squadron, calls the shots as a Joint Direct Attack Munitions (JDAM) is offloaded from the bomb bay of a B-2A Spirit. The bomber was reloaded with a different configuration to fly a combat sortie in support of Operation Iraqi Freedom. *Air Force/509th BW*

BOTTOM LEFT: Seldom used, but still in the inventory, is the 5,000-pound laser guided GBU-28 "Bunker Buster" that was used successfully during Desert Storm utilizing F-111s and F-15Es. *James C. Goodall*

BOTTOM CENTER: The 5,000-pound laser-guided GBU-28 "Bunker Buster" without its distinctive laser-guiding nosepiece. *James C. Goodall*

BOTTOM RIGHT: The replacement for the GBU-28 and its laser-guided system is the GBU-37/B (GAM 113), a 5,000 pound class GPS-guided weapon that doesn't require a visual clue or laser to pinpoint the location to strike. *James C. Goodall*

LEFT: As in all wars, weapons loaders and ground crews love to send messages to the enemy. Here are three examples of the "Messages from Above" via the B-2As from the weapons loading crew on the British Protectorate, the Island of Diego Garcia, located in the middle of the Indian Ocean during the hunt for Osama Bin Laden. *Author's collection*

RIGHT: SrA Stephanie Lopez straps a joint-direct attack munitions that will be loaded on to a bomb-lift vehicle. She is a weapons loader with the 40th Expeditionary Maintenance Squadron at a forward-deployed location and is from Minot Air Force Base, ND. *Air Force/509th BW*

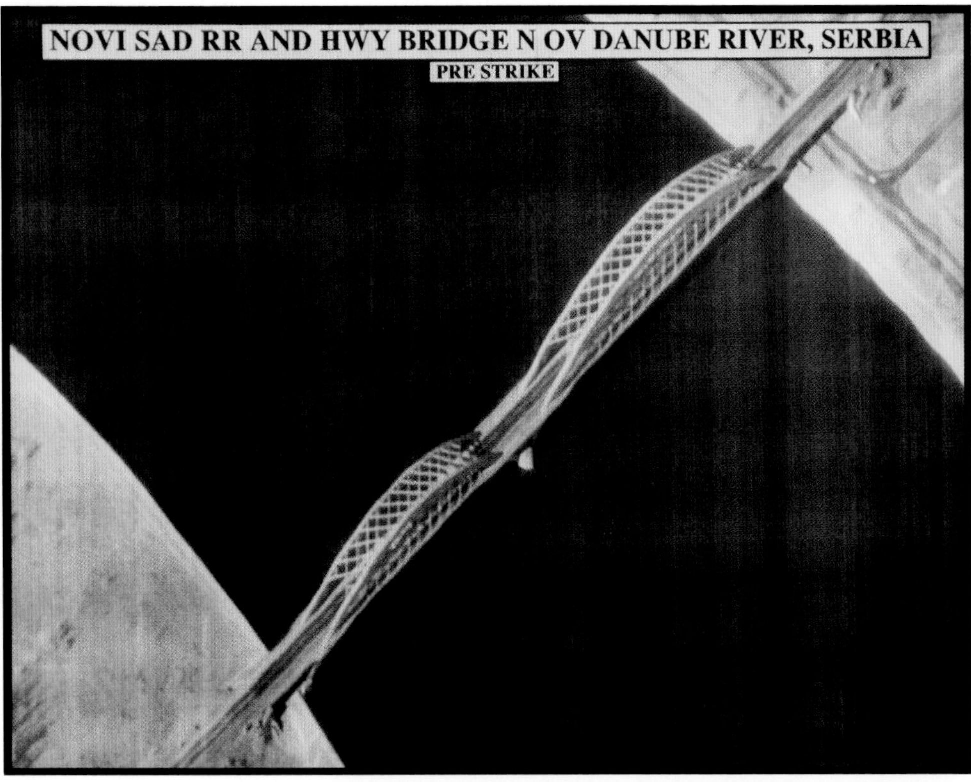

TOP LEFT AND RIGHT: During a May 2002 interview with Majors Tony Monetti and Harry Foster, the question was asked as to just how good were the radar images from the Hughes (now Raytheon) APQ-181 low probability of intercept radar. Their answer was "photographic quality." Here are two examples of just how good the Hughes system really is. These images were de-graded in order to allow the images to be made public.

This is a "before" and "after" view, taken from above 40,000 feet, in total darkness and with cloud cover of the Novi Sad RR and Highway bridge crossing over the Danube River, Serbia. Tony said that an F-15E Strike Eagle dropped two GBU-15s with zero results. Along came an F-117A and dropped two GBU-27s: still nothing. The B-2A still had eight GBU-32s left in its weapons bay. Seven were targeted on the center span and just for good measure; number eight was targeted at the shore end of the north span. *Air Force/509th BW*

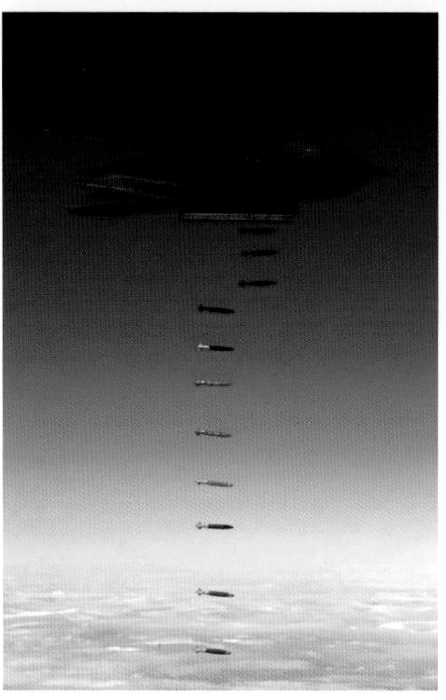

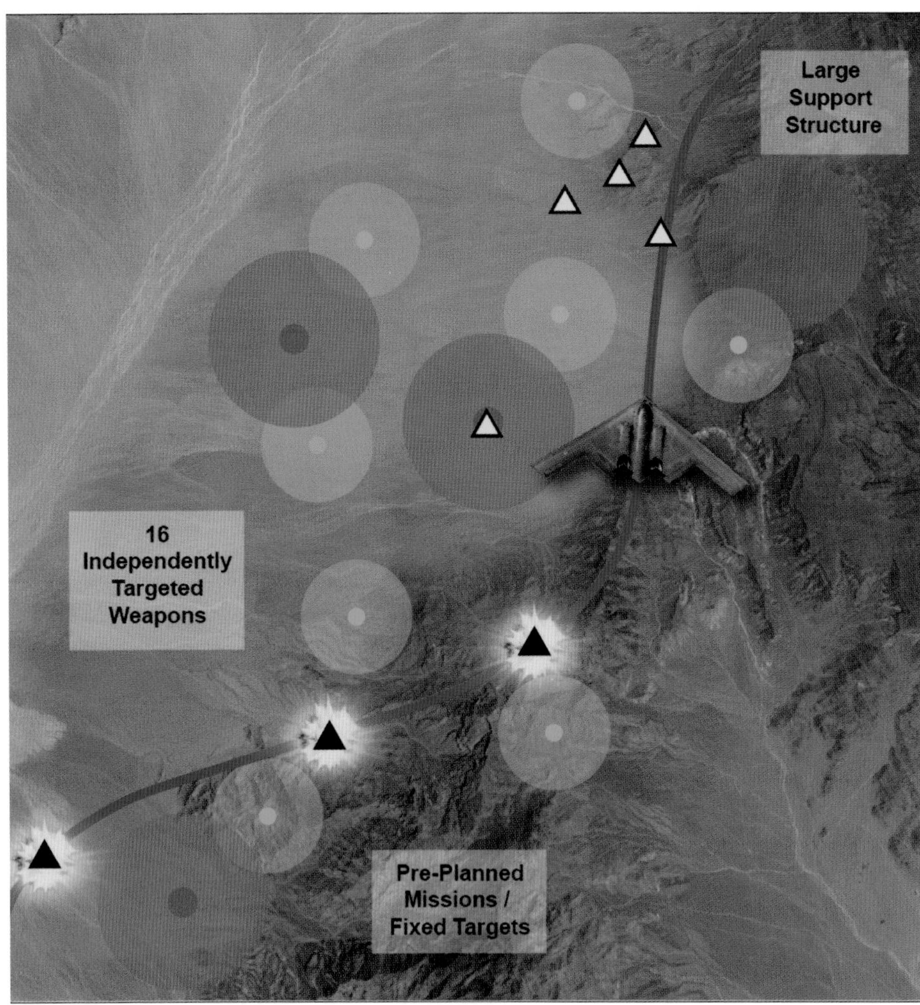

TOP LEFT: The Blue Line is a key part of stealth tactics. Tactics are just as vital as the airplane's design and the secret materials that reduce its radar cross-section. Uniquely crafted for each mission, the Blue Line stitches the assigned targets onto a flight path calculated to avoid the most dangerous enemy defenses. Surviving a mission depends on detailed planning before takeoff. *Northrop Grumman*

RIGHT: High-quality images of Battle Damage Assessment from a bomb run over the Serbian support base in Kirvovo, and the Kragjevac armament and motor vehicle plant, Crvena Zastava, Serbia. If you look closely, there are eight different holes in eight different buildings. The results of one B-2A. One B-2A today with 500-pound smart bombs can do the damage of 1,500 B-17s in World War II, all because of the precision and the ability to target the correct area. *Air Force/509th BW*

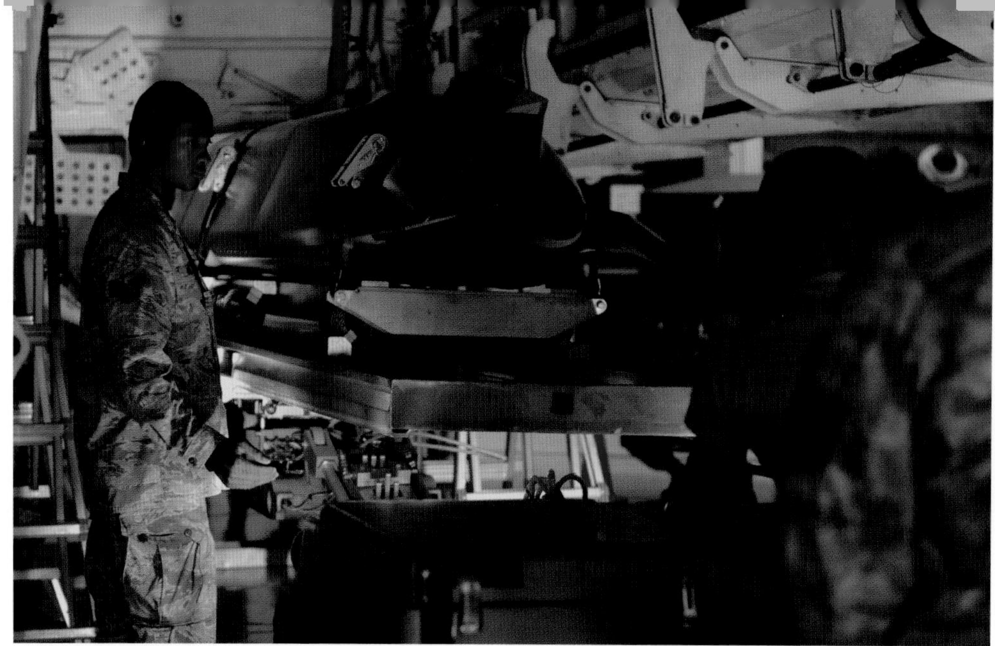

AGM-158 JASSM (Joint Air-to-Surface Standoff Missile)

TOP LEFT: Each AGM-158 JASSM (Joint-Air-to-Surface-Standoff-Missile) is loaded on its secure spring-mounted pallet. Not only does this technique protect the JASSM, it makes loading the weapon much easier. *James C. Goodall*

BOTTOM LEFT: When in storage or in transport, each JASSM comes in its own secure container. The pallet has provisions that make the entire package very easy to transport in addition to protecting it from the elements. *James C. Goodall*

TOP RIGHT: SrA Keandre Lowe guides A1C Daniel Rexius, and the practice munitions he is transporting, into place during a load crew of the quarter competition at Whiteman Air Force Base, MO, July 18, 2013. The load crew competition uses practice munitions and a mock B-2A Spirit to simulate real-world loading conditions. Both airmen are load crew team members from the 13th Aircraft Maintenance Unit.
Air Force/509th BW

BOTTOM RIGHT: Still mounted on its transportable pallet, the JASSM is already properly balanced and secured to its shock-mounted cradle. Shown here is the way the JASSM is moved from the weapons trailer via one MHU-83C/E Munitions Loading System to another in preparation for loading.
Air Force/509th BW

TOP LEFT: Joint Air-to-Surface Standard Missile (JASSM), manufactured by Lockheed Martin, drops from the weapons bay of the B-2A *Spirit of Texas,* AV-7 (88-0328), toward a target several hundred miles away. *Air Force/509th BW*

BOTTOM LEFT: The AGM-158 JASSM is an autonomous, long-range missile developed and produced by Lockheed Martin. This conventional, air-to-ground and precision standoff missile was designed primarily for the US Air Force. The 2,000-pound class weapon offers high capability and precision in destroying stationary as well as relocatable targets. *Air Force/509th BW*

RIGHT: JASSM striking a target in the Utah test range. *Lockheed Martin*

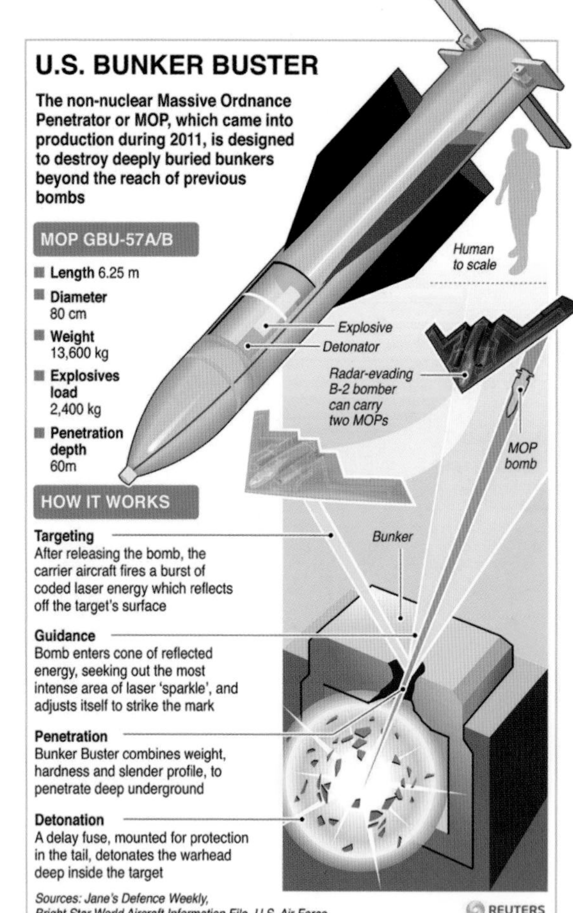

Mother of All Bombs ... a.k.a. MOAB!

TOP LEFT: In June 2007, Northrop Grumman was awarded a contract to integrate the Boeing 30,000-pound Massive Ordnance Penetrator (MOP) weapon on the B-2A. The MOP is GPS-guided, contains 2,400kg (5,300lb) of explosive, and is designed to penetrate hardened, deeply buried targets. The B-2A is capable of carrying two MOP weapons, one in each weapons bay. *Jim Mumaw*

TOP CENTER: Reuters infographic on the MOP. *Jane's Defense Weekly*

TOP RIGHT: Prototype GBU-43/B Massive Ordnance Penetrator an instant before impact on Eglin AFB's Range 70. *Air Force/509th BW*

BOTTOM RIGHT: The MOP is described as "a powerful new bomb aimed squarely at the underground nuclear facilities of Iran and North Korea." The gargantuan bomb is longer than eleven persons standing shoulder-to-shoulder (or more than twenty feet base to nose). *Boeing*

Nuclear Deterrent in the Form of the B83, and the B61 Family of Nuclear Weapons.

TOP AND MIDDLE LEFT: View of a flight-test body of a B61-12 nuclear weapon, used for testing on operational aircraft at the Sandia National Laboratories in Albuquerque, New Mexico on April 2, 2015. The flight-test body is a semi-operational copy of an actual B61-12 but without the "physics package" (nuclear bomb) or functional tail fins. *Jerry Redfern*

BOTTOM LEFT: Maintenance technicians prepare a B61-12 nuclear weapon test to study the effects of separation from the Boeing F-15E, the Lockheed Martin F-16, and the "Beast," the mighty B-2 Spirit. *USAF photo*

RIGHT: Members of a weapons load crew move a load trailer into position under the bomb bay of a B-2 Spirit at Whiteman AFB, MO. The weapons load is part of the 72nd Test and Evaluation Squadron's Combat Sledgehammer. *USAF photo*

TOP LEFT: A head-on view of the four nuclear weapons to be loaded in the B-2A's weapons bay. The smaller of the two types of weapons is the B61-11. About fifty B61-11 bombs are in the operational stockpile. This weapon is the newest in the US arsenal. First originated in 1993, the Mod 11 is designed as a "bunker buster," and capable of attacking hardened targets underground. The Mod 11 is designed to penetrate targets before exploding, and thus in theory does not need as large a yield to fulfill its mission. The B61-11 has a variable yield of 0.3 to 340 kilotons. *Air Force/509th BW*

TOP RIGHT: The MHU-204/M Munitions Lifting Trailer is used to lift the Advanced Rotary Launcher, with weapons already attached, up and into the weapons bay of the B-2A Spirit. *James C. Goodall*

MIDDLE LEFT: With the help of several spotters, a munitions specialist of the 509th Munitions Squadron makes the final positioning commands to a Rotary Launcher Erector under the bomb bay of a B-2A Spirit, October 27, 1997, during exercise Global Guardian. This is one of two Rotary Launcher Assemblies loaded with multiple (actual) nuclear weapons. *Air Force/509th BW*

BOTTOM LEFT: It's not very often that the USAF will publish photos of the loading of actual nuclear weapons, however, during exercise Global Guardian they did. This crew loaded two B83 Mod 1 high-yield nuclear weapons, and one B63-11 deep penetrator version of the B63-7. Some 600 B83 warheads are in the arsenal, with about 480 available to operational long-range bombers such as the B-2A Spirit. An upgraded version, designated as B83 Mod 1, began production in FY1999. *Air Force/509th BW*

TOP LEFT: Munitions specialists of the 509th Munitions Squadron control a Rotary Launcher Erector under the aft section of a B-2A Spirit, during exercise Global Guardian. This is one of two Rotary Launcher Assemblies, loaded with multiple (actual) nuclear weapons that will be raised and mounted in to the bomb bays. *Air Force/509th BW*

TOP CENTER: A close-up view of control unit used by munitions specialist of the 509th Munitions Squadron which controls a Rotary Launcher Erector under the aft section of a B-2A Spirit, during exercise Global Guardian. *Air Force/509th BW*

TOP RIGHT: B-2A Spirit Weapons Layout. *Air Force/509th BW*

BOTTOM RIGHT: The most powerful quiver in the B-2A's arsenal is its nuclear capability. Pictured here is the standard B-61-7. Next in line is the real big punch, the B-83 Mod 1 thermonuclear weapon. The 2,400-pound B-83 has a selectable yield up to 1.2 megatons, and the B-2A can carry up to sixteen of these. The last weapon on the trailer is the deep penetrator B-61-11. This is a modified version of the B-61-7 that is in the current Air Force inventory. With a length of eleven feet, 9.5 inches, the B-61-11 weighs in at around 720 pounds, and has a selected yield from 0.3 kilotons to 340 kilotons. *James C. Goodall*

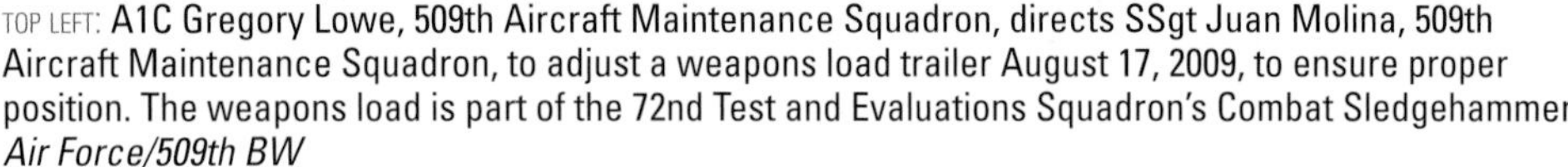

TOP LEFT: A1C Gregory Lowe, 509th Aircraft Maintenance Squadron, directs SSgt Juan Molina, 509th Aircraft Maintenance Squadron, to adjust a weapons load trailer August 17, 2009, to ensure proper position. The weapons load is part of the 72nd Test and Evaluations Squadron's Combat Sledgehammer. *Air Force/509th BW*

TOP RIGHT: Members of the 393rd Bomb Squadron cautiously raise weapons into the bomb bay in the belly of the B-2A Spirit in support of a United States Strategic Command Exercise on Whiteman AFB, MO. The rotary launch assembly is being lifted into a B-2A utilizing MHU-204/M Munitions Lifting Trailer during the August 17, 2009, training exercise. This inspection is one of the first inspections to fall under Global Strike Command since it has stood up. *Air Force/509th BW*

BOTTOM RIGHT: TSgt Damen Cipolla, 509th Aircraft Maintenance Squadron, inspects the rotary launch assembly as its being lifted into a B-2A, as Senior Airman Lowe runs the controls to lift the assembly into place, August 17, 2009. *Air Force/509th BW*

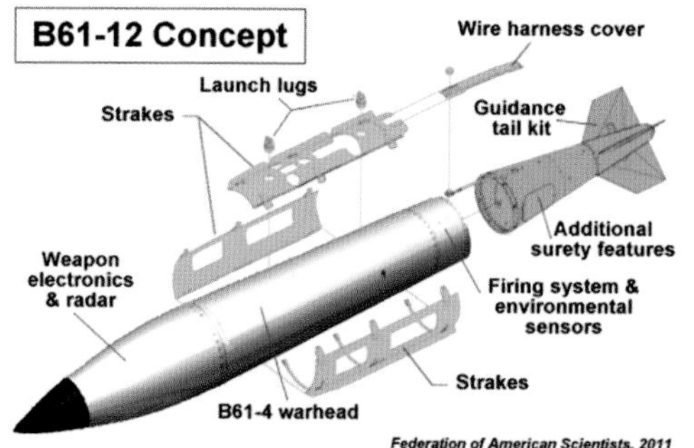

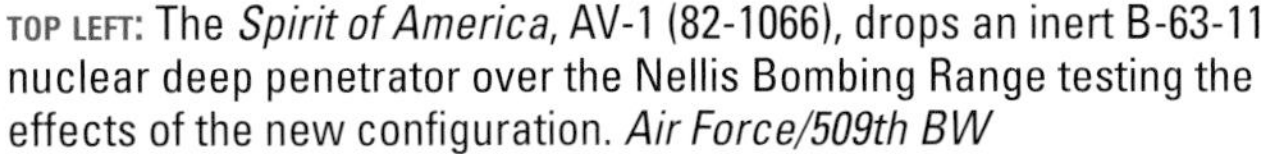

TOP LEFT: The *Spirit of America*, AV-1 (82-1066), drops an inert B-63-11 nuclear deep penetrator over the Nellis Bombing Range testing the effects of the new configuration. *Air Force/509th BW*

TOP CENTER: In order to stabilize the B-63-11, and to improve accuracy, the weapon has a gas generator that once released from the weapons bay of the B-2, causes the weapon to spin (like the rifling in a gun barrel causes the bullet to go where aimed). *Air Force/509th BW*

TOP RIGHT: B63-12 concept layout. *Federation of American Scientists*

BOTTOM RIGHT: A close up view of the B-63-11 training shape at the Whiteman AFB weapons training section. *James C. Goodall*

TOP LEFT: As you look down the leading edge of the *Spirit of Nebraska*, AV-13 (89-0128), you see what looks like bands or clips. This is an indicator that the B-2A in question was a "Block 20" and not fully mission-capable. *James C. Goodall*

BOTTOM LEFT: Another view of the *Spirit of Pennsylvania*, AV-20 (93-1087). The leading edge is smooth and is an indication that this B-2A is at least at "Block 30" standards, and is fully mission-capable. By the year 2000, all B-2A Spirits had been upgraded to full "Block 30" standards. *James C. Goodall* **TOP RIGHT:** A1C Eljay Noel, 13th Aircraft Maintenance Unit B-2A Spirit crew chief, marshals B-2A *Spirit of America*, AV-1 (82-1066), out of its protective hangar prior to its departure to Smoky Hill Air National Guard Range in Salina, KS, to participate in Global Strike Challenge on June 26, 2012. *Air Force/509th BW*

BOTTOM CENTER: On November 1, 2009, two B-2A Spirits, the *Spirit of Arizona*, AV-2 (82-1067), and the *Spirit of Nebraska*, AV-13 (89-0128), on the taxiway at RAF Fairford waiting its turn to take off. *Laurie Hughes*

BOTTOM RIGHT: The *Spirit of Missouri*, AV-8 (88-0329), on the ramp at Whitman AFB, MO, during engine run-up after engine change. *Air Force/509th BW*

LEFT: Close up detail of the main landing gear on the B-2A Spirit. On the prototype B-2, the *Spirit of America*, AV-1 (82-1066), Northrop Grumman used a modified set of Boeing 767 landing gear. Once it was decided to convert AV-1 into a fully mission-capable bomber, the gear was changed out. *James C. Goodall*

RIGHT: Looking up into the cavernous main gear wheel well gives the onlooker a perspective of just how thick the wing of the B-2A really is. The over-sized wheel well also allows for access into the outer wing assembly without the need for an external opening. *James C. Goodall*

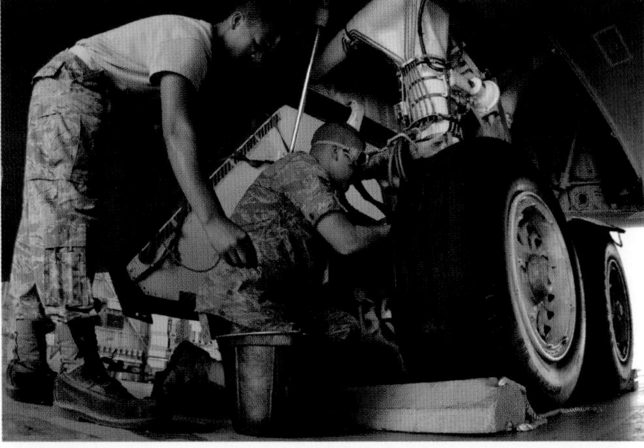

TOP LEFT: As on all large aircraft, changing a tire or bleeding the brake line is not a job for one person. Everything on the B-2A is big and complex. Here a maintenance technician prepares to bleed a hydraulic line on the B-2A's massive landing gear. *Air Force/509th BW*

TOP CENTER: While on rotation to Andersen AFB, Guam, the *Spirit of Pennsylvania*, AV-20 (93-1087), was in need of a tire change in one of Andersen's many revetments. As of this writing, Andersen still is in need of more hangar space for large aircraft maintenance such as the B-2A Spirit. *Air Force/509th BW*

BOTTOM LEFT: Looking up into the B-2A's wheel well located to the front and outside is the APU Permanent Magnet Generator System, or PMG. A PMG is mounted on the start motor drive shaft in each APU. This system provides 28 Volts DC power to the B-2A. *James C. Goodall*

TOP RIGHT: A1C Benjamin Feldkamp works on the brakes of a B-2A Spirit August 22, 2009, at Whiteman Air Force Base, MO. Airman Feldkamp and other 509th Aircraft Maintenance Squadron crew chiefs work around the clock to ensure the B-2A is mission-ready at all times. *Air Force/509th BW*

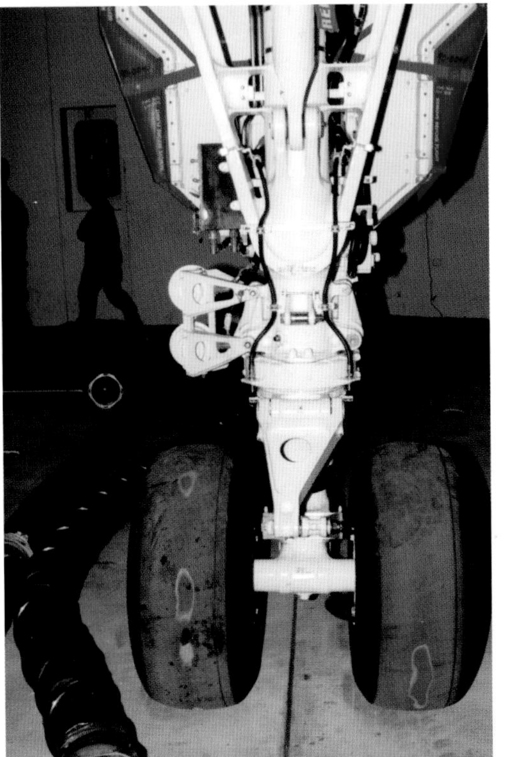

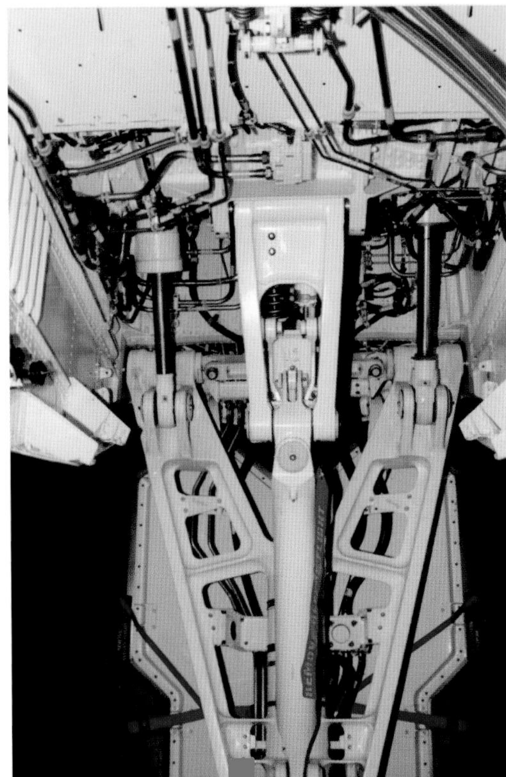

TOP LEFT: 509th Bomb Wing maintenance crew checks out hydraulic leakage on the nose gear of the *Spirit of America*, AV-1 (82-1066), in one of Whiteman's many dedicated B-2A hangars. *Air Force/509th BW*

BOTTOM LEFT: The backside of the B-2A's nose wheel assembly. *James C. Goodall*

BOTTOM CENTER: Looking up and forward into the B-2A's nose gear assembly showing the hydraulic actuators, gear retract linkage, and the complex mechanism needed to support the 376,000 lb. (170,600 kg) maximum gross weight of the B-2A Spirit. *James C. Goodall*

TOP RIGHT: A side view of the B-2A's nose landing gear and wheel assembly. Located just above the nose landing lights and below the four-digit serial number are the controls for opening the crew access ladder. *James C. Goodall*

TOP LEFT: On the port side of the nose wheel well is one of the many access panels that allow entry into the airframe without the need for external opening that might affect the LO signature of the B-2A Spirit. *James C. Goodall*

RIGHT: At the rear and starboard side of the nose wheel well are several more access panels. At the very rear of the wheel well, in addition to the access panels is an emergency crew access door handle (the yellow and black stripped lever on the starboard side of the wheel well) that can manually open the crew door and stairs. *James C. Goodall*

BOTTOM LEFT: Head-on view of the nose landing gear door. It is on this door that the crews names are stenciled and as well as the "DCC" or dedicated crew chief and their assistants, plus the last five digits of the B-2A serial number. From the beginning of the war on terror, all crewmember names have been removed to prevent retaliation by Islamic extremists. *James C. Goodall*

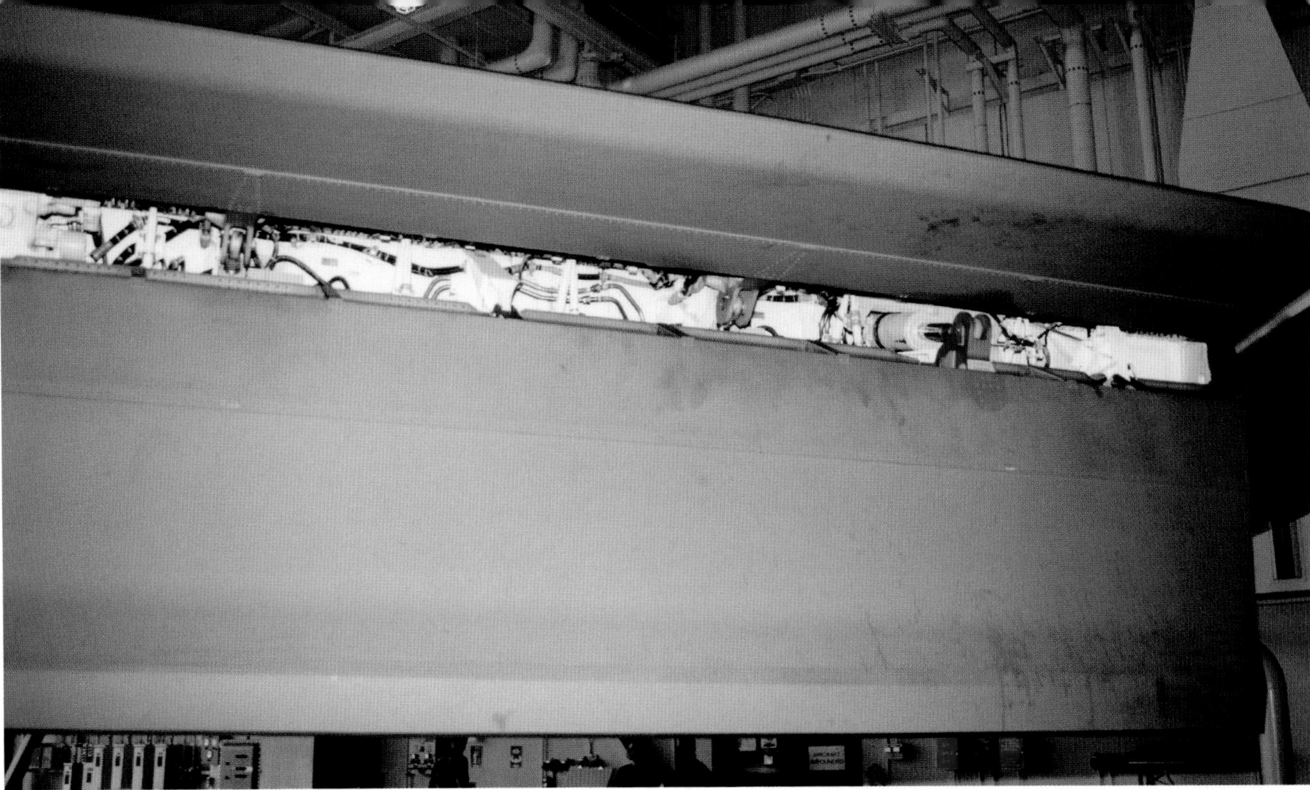

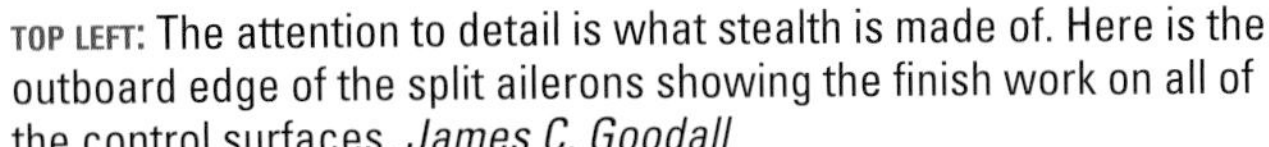

TOP LEFT: The attention to detail is what stealth is made of. Here is the outboard edge of the split ailerons showing the finish work on all of the control surfaces. *James C. Goodall*

TOP RIGHT: Looking up into the linkage and hydraulic rams that control the B-2A's control surfaces. This is the only place you can see the inner workings of the B-2As flaps and ailerons. *James C. Goodall*

BOTTOM RIGHT: Even the B-2A's anti-collision lights retract when the B-2A goes into harm's way. As with every other surface on the B-2A, the cap on the top of the formation light is diamond-shaped and once retracted, does not give a reflective surface. *James C. Goodall*

TOP LEFT: A view from below, looking down the leading of the *Spirit of America*, AV-1 (82-1066), showing the unique shape to the leading edge. *James C. Goodall*

BOTTOM LEFT: The one-piece movable "Beaver Tail" in a full down position. The tail assembly is used for takeoffs and landings to control the angle of attack, or AOA, and at low level for the reduction of airframe shake, rattle, and roll. *James C. Goodall*

RIGHT: Two more views of Northrop's patented split ailerons used to control yaw on the earlier Northrop flying wings—the XB-35 and YB-49—and now on the B-2As. *James C. Goodall*

A night view of the flight line at Whiteman AFB, MO looking under the *Spirit of Georgia*, AV-14 (89-0129). The *Spirit of California*, AV-9 (88-0330), in the background. *Air Force/509th BW*

B-2 Spirit Cockpit P6 Mod

What the B-2A's cockpit looks today. There are several different configurations since the B-2A first took to the air. The cockpit has evolved from the early Block 10 cockpits through the Block 20, the Block 30, and the P5 to its current P6 configuration. *Air Force/509th BW*

Early B-2 Simulator Pre-Block 30

One can't notice much change between the two cockpits. The major change was from the early tube-type multifunction displays (MFD) to touch-screen LED MFDs. Today's P6 qualified B-2A crews would have a hard time in transitioning backward, even to a "Block 30" standard cockpit. *Air Force/509th BW*

TOP LEFT: On the port side of the B-2A's cockpit is the command pilot's set of throttles. Lighting controls are placed aft and outboard of the throttles. The toggle switch in front of and outboard of the throttles operates the auxiliary engine air intakes. The "Consent" panel is for weapons release, with "Conventional Release Enable," or as shown in this photo, the "Conv Rel Enable" switch. The next two red switch protectors are for the release of nuclear weapons: shown under the "NUC" label are "Unlk Enbl," or Unlock Nuke Enable, and "PA Enbl." *James C. Goodall*

BOTTOM LEFT: Looking over the pilot's ejection seat are the four MFDs, the B-2A's control stick, and on the far right is the landing gear retract/released lever. *James C. Goodall*

TOP RIGHT: A full-on view of the lighting and communications panel on the outboard side of the pilot's side of the cockpit. The three red rectangles next to the "Remove Before Flight" flag are the landing gear up/down and locked indicators. *James C. Goodall*

TOP: On the mission commander's side of the cockpit are some of the same controls found on the pilot's side: communications panel and the same "Consent" panel for weapons release. The control stick mounted on the forward console is the weapons systems cursor control. This unit updates the Global Positioning System (GPS)-guided weapons in conjunction with the high-resolution Hughes (now Raytheon) AN/ALQ-181 radar. *James C. Goodall*

BOTTOM RIGHT: Both Spirit crewmen use a floor-mounted control stick. The large gray button on the black control stick top activates control system trim, while the smaller red button beside the trim switch releases the weapons. *James C. Goodall*

B-2A Cockpit Layout

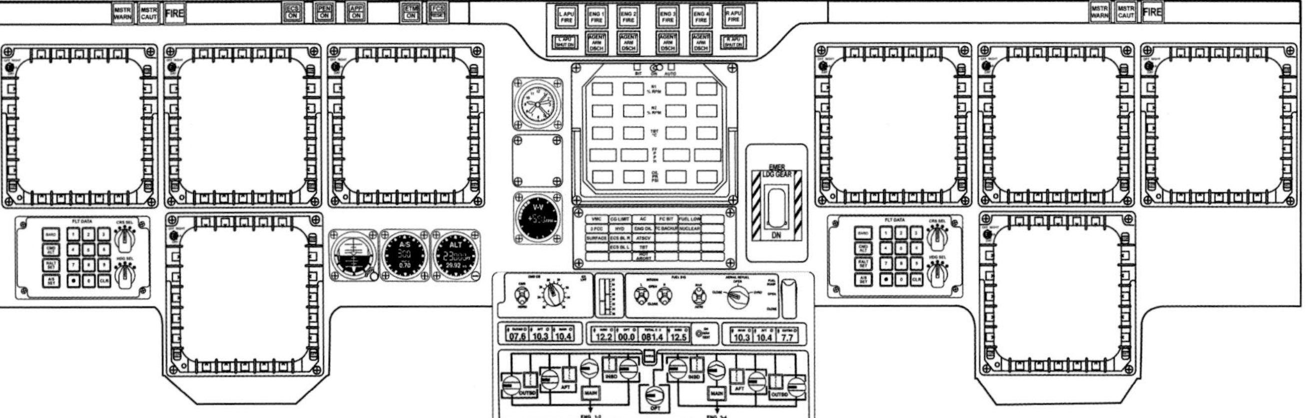

TOP LEFT: The B-2A's main instrument panel layout. *Author's collection*

BOTTOM LEFT: The center console of the B-2A's cockpit with the mission commander's throttle quadrant. On the right below is the weapon's "Jettison" master control switches. On the far left is the "Ejection Sequence" selector, pilots' navigation input panel, and various other cockpit command functions. *James C. Goodall*

BOTTOM CENTER: Overall view of the main instrument panel on the B-2A shows the multiple touchscreen multifunction displays—four for each crew member—and the pilot's navigation input screen mounted on the forward port side of the center console with the weapons ejection controls. The bleed air panel is aft of the navigation panel. *James C. Goodall*

BOTTOM RIGHT: The overhead panel controls the opening and closing of the crew access door, all external lighting, engine stop and start switches, and both APU start/stop controls *James C. Goodall*

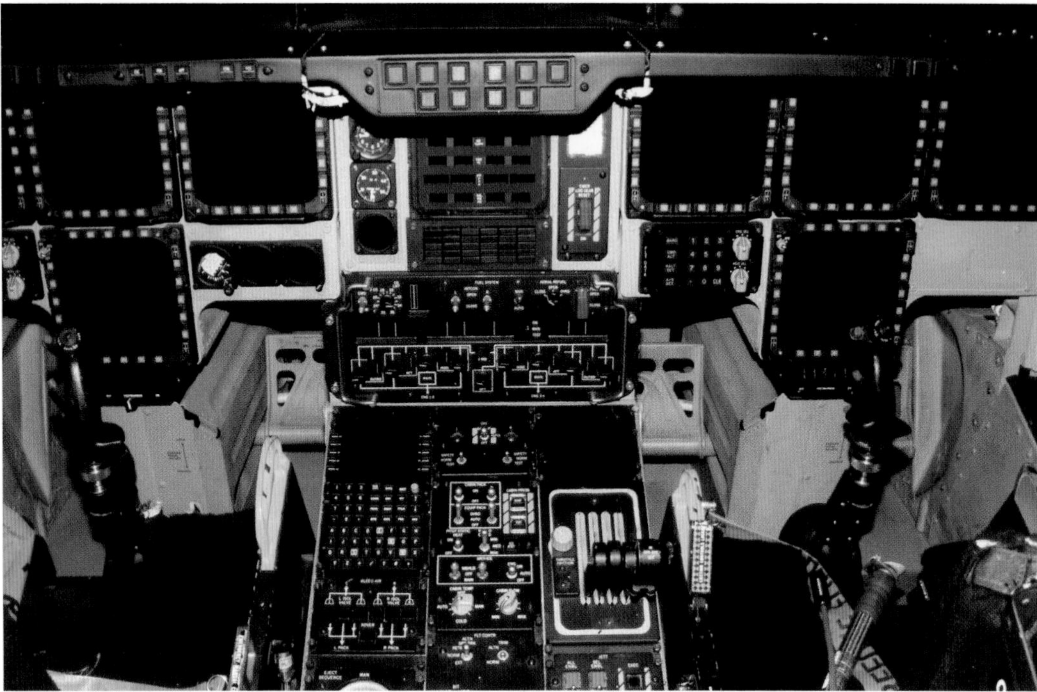

AC / DC CIRCUIT BREAKER PANEL LOCATIONS

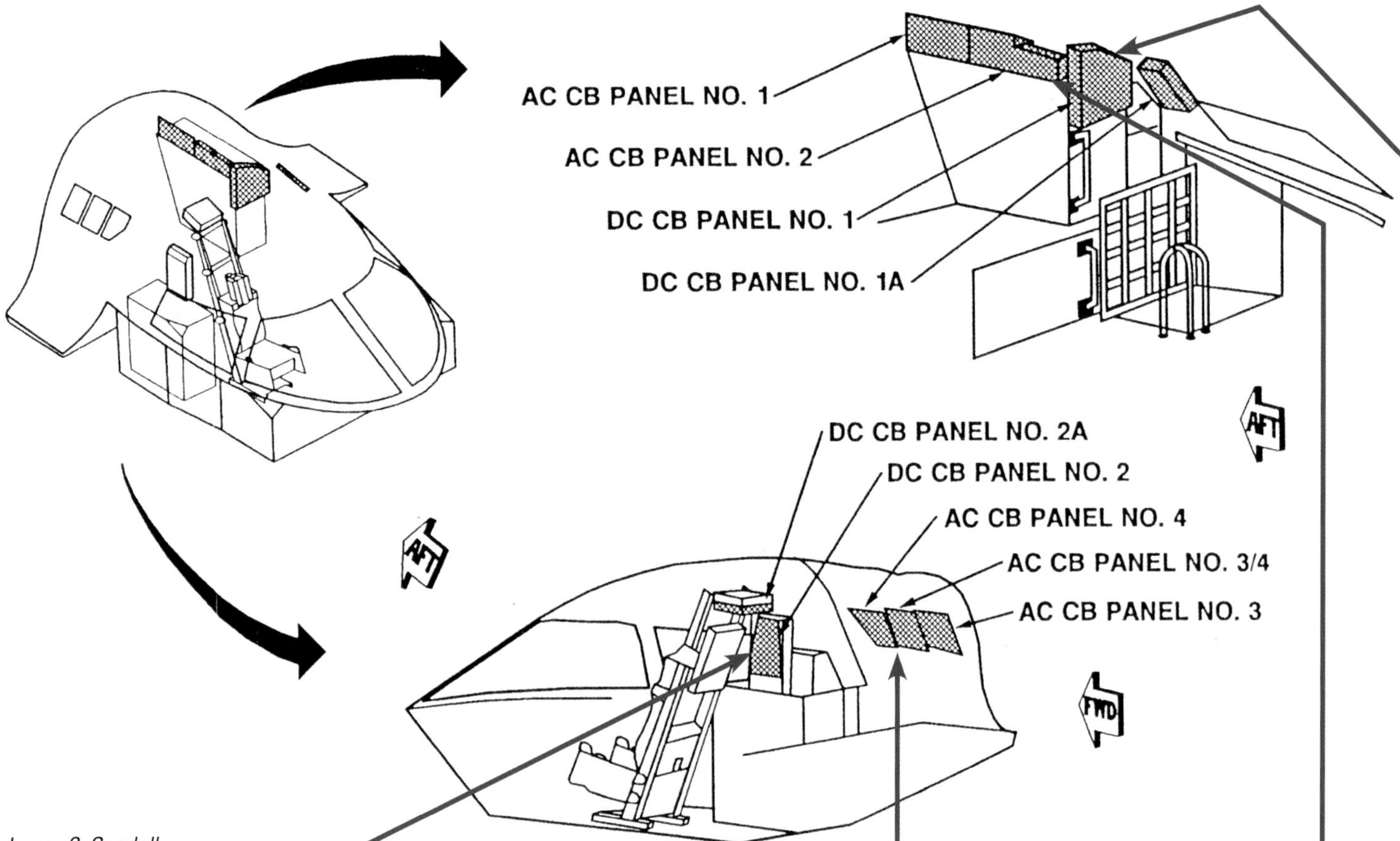

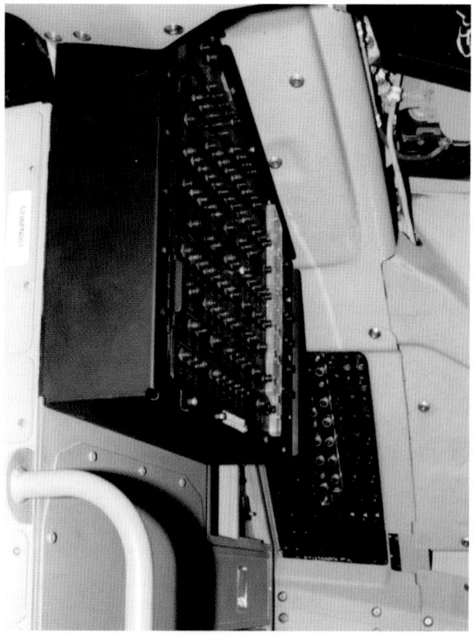

AC CB PANEL NO. 1
AC CB PANEL NO. 2
DC CB PANEL NO. 1
DC CB PANEL NO. 1A

AFT

DC CB PANEL NO. 2A
DC CB PANEL NO. 2
AC CB PANEL NO. 4
AC CB PANEL NO. 3/4
AC CB PANEL NO. 3

AFT
FWD

James C. Goodall

B-2.7

AIRCRAFT ENTRY - Continued

B-2

T.O. 00-105E-9

2. MANUAL ENTRY

WARNING

Do not enter nose wheel well unless the aft nose gear door safety pin is installed.

NOTE:
Electrical and hydraulic power must be available to open nose gear door.

a. MANUAL ENTRY DOOR ACCESS
(1) Place nose gear door switch to OPEN.
(2) After aft nose gear door opens, install aft nose gear door safety pin (P/N DAA 7252G012-005).
(3) Manually rotate ALTERNATE DOOR UNLOCK lever on the aft bulkhead of nose wheel well to OPEN. Return lever to NEUTRAL. Substantial force is required to pull the lever. Outer crew entry door opens partially and exposes door edge. Carefully pull down to full open and manually extend crew entry ladder.

b. ENTER AIRCRAFT

WARNING

To prevent injury to personnel, maintain positive control of lower ladder. Ladder will retract slightly if released.

(1) Remove safety pin (P/N DAA7200G005-001) from safety pin stowage, located under third step from top of ladder, and install in ladder at bottom third step on right side.
(2) Install blade seal protectors if available.
(3) Climb crew entry ladder to inner crew entry door, turn door handle clockwise 180 degrees, push door, until it latches in the open position. Door could be difficult to push against cabin pressurization if engines are running.

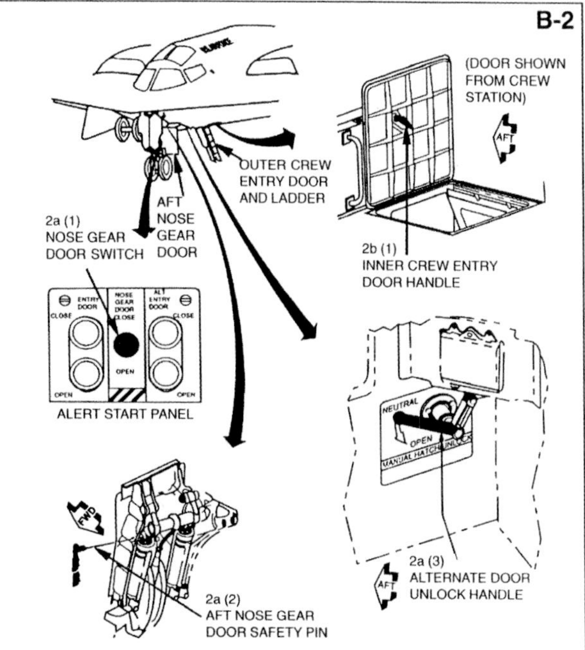

TOP LEFT: Illustration from an unclassified B-2A tech order. *Author's collection*

BOTTOM LEFT: Inside the cockpit looking down the crew access ladder. *James C. Goodall*

BOTTOM CENTER: Looking up from the ground at the crew access ladder and hatch in the closed position. *James C. Goodall*

BOTTOM RIGHT: From inside the B-2A's cockpit looking down at the crew access hatch in the closed and locked position. On the very long 24- to 44-hour missions, it is in this area that the crew will open up their "Wal-Mart" styled fold-up beach lounge, and roll out their sleeping bags for a brief, but needed, sleep on long missions. *James C. Goodall*

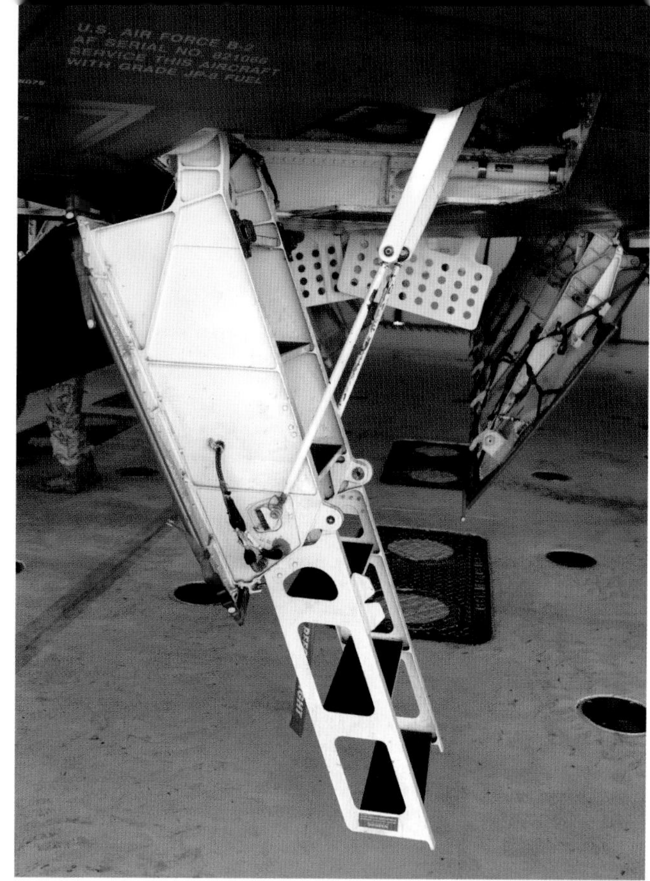

TOP: Three views of the B-2A's cockpit access stairs The bottom part of the crew ladder is usually opened by the ground crew and is pinned in the open position when in use. The hatch cover has the usual B-2A-styled saw-tooth edge. *James C. Goodall*

BOTTOM LEFT: Aircraft entry controls are mounted on the B-2A Spirit's nose wheel assembly. *James C. Goodall*

BOTTOM RIGHT: Illustration from an unclassified B-2A tech order. *Author's collection*

B-2.6

T.O. 00-105E-9

AIRCRAFT ENTRY

NOTE:
Aircraft entry is through the crew entry door on the left side of the aircraft.

WARNING

Door opening areas must be cleared of personnel and equipment before opening either crew entry or aft nose gear door.

1. NORMAL ENTRY

a. NORMAL ENTRY DOOR ACCESS

(1) Push either the ENTRY DOOR OPEN switch on the alert start panel, OR pull the ALT ENTRY DOOR UNLOCK lever, in the nose-wheel well aft bulkhead. Return lever to NEUTRAL. Door opens within fifteen seconds.

b. ENTER AIRCRAFT

WARNING

To prevent injury to personnel, maintain positive control of lower ladder. Ladder will retract slightly if released.

(1) Pull lower ladder to full down position.

(2) Remove safety pin (P/N DAA7200G005 -001) from safety pin stowage, located under third step from top of ladder, and install in ladder at bottom third step on right side.

(3) Install blade seal protectors if available.

(4) Climb crew entry ladder to inner crew entry door, turn door handle clockwise 180 degrees, push door, until it latches in the open position. Door could be difficult to push against cabin pressurization if engines are running.

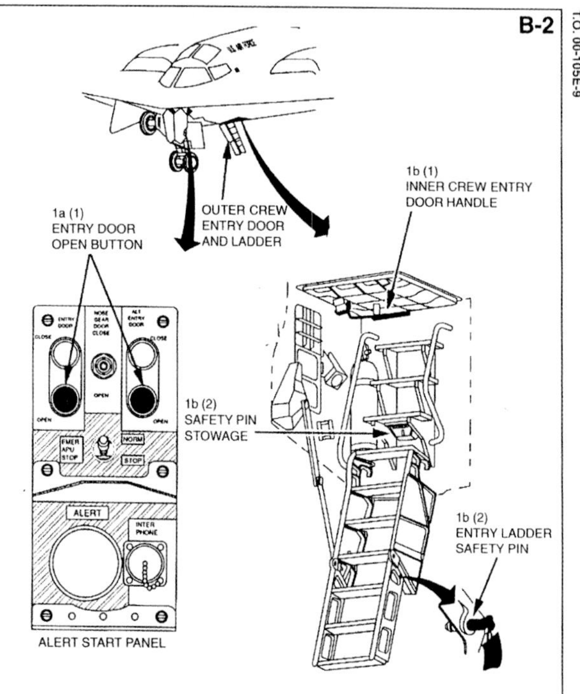

On the Ramp

The flight line at Nellis AFB, NV, during a Red Flag exercise with around ten billion dollars worth of B-2As all lined up and ready to go. From front to rear are the *Spirit of Nebraska*, AV-13 (89-0128), the *Spirit of Arizona*, AV-2 (82-1087), the *Spirit of Hawaii*, AV-16 (90-0041), and the *Spirit of Louisiana*, AV-21 (93-1088). *Don Logan*

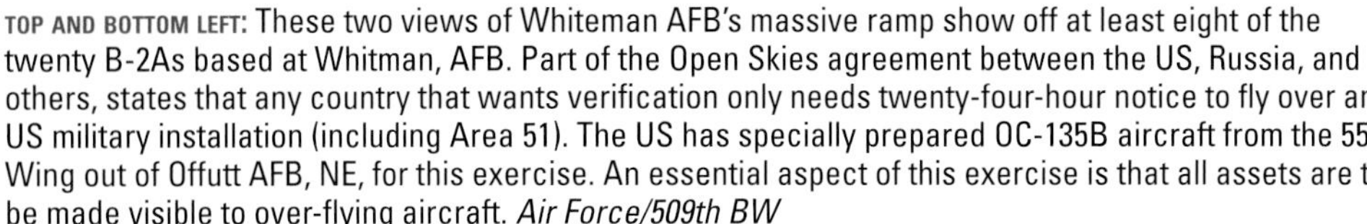

TOP AND BOTTOM LEFT: These two views of Whiteman AFB's massive ramp show off at least eight of the twenty B-2As based at Whitman, AFB. Part of the Open Skies agreement between the US, Russia, and others, states that any country that wants verification only needs twenty-four-hour notice to fly over any US military installation (including Area 51). The US has specially prepared OC-135B aircraft from the 55th Wing out of Offutt AFB, NE, for this exercise. An essential aspect of this exercise is that all assets are to be made visible to over-flying aircraft. *Air Force/509th BW*

TOP RIGHT: Two B-2A Bombers taxi down Taxiway Delta on March 4, 2008, marking the end of Whiteman's first Nuclear Operational Readiness Exercise (NORE) for that year. The NORE is in preparation of the combined Nuclear Surety Inspection and Nuclear Operational Readiness Inspection (NORI) from May 29 through June 11, 2008. *Air Force/509th BW*

BOTTOM RIGHT: Six B-2s, with the *Spirit of Louisiana*, AV-21 (93-1087), the closest B-2, prepare for a quick response takeoff exercise during Whiteman's first Nuclear Operational Readiness Exercise on March 5, 2008. *Air Force/509th BW*

TOP: Three B-2A Spirits on the Whiteman ramp, with engines running; the *Spirit of New York*, AV-3 (82-1068), *Spirit of Texas*, AV-7 (88-0328), and *Spirit of Ohio*, AV-5 (82-1070) are readied for a long-range training exercise on April 8, 2014. *Air Force/509th BW*

MIDDLE LEFT: Three B-2A Spirits taxi down the Andersen AFB flight line preparing for a quick launch at one-minute intervals, on August 18, 2005. The B-2As and 270 personnel from Whiteman AFB, MO, were deployed to Andersen as part of the Pacific Command's continuous bomber presence in the Asia-Pacific region, enhancing regional security and the US's commitment to the Western Pacific. *Air Force/509th BW*

MIDDLE RIGHT: SrA Mindy High prepares to launch a B-2A Spirit bomber during a mission at Andersen Air Force Base, Guam. The B-2As deployed to Andersen AFB on February 25, 2005, provide US Pacific Command officials a continuous bomber presence in the Asia-Pacific region. *Air Force/509th BW*

BOTTOM LEFT: Three B-2s, the *Spirit of Alaska*, AV-15 (90-0040), the *Spirit of America*, AV-1 (82-1066), and the *Spirit of Georgia*, AV-14 (89-0129), wait on the Whiteman ramp in preparation of a multi-plane training mission. *Air Force/509th BW*

TOP LEFT: B-2 Spirit crew chiefs, SrA Jeremy Pratt (left) and SSgt David Rohde (right), wait for the pilots to finish pre-flight checklists of their B-2, the *Spirit of Arizona*, AV-2 (82-1067), at Whiteman AFB on April 2, 2003. Both crew chiefs are there to ensure the bomber is ready to fly on a combat mission over Iraq in support of Operation Iraqi Freedom. *Air Force/509th BW*

BOTTOM LEFT: A B-2A Spirit, assigned to the 509th Bomb Wing (BW), taxis out on a mission, and is the first-ever deployed to this forward operating location in support of Operation Enduring Freedom. *Air Force/509th BW*

TOP RIGHT: An unidentified pilot waits to climb into a B-2, the *Spirit of Alaska*, AV-15 (90-0041), as it waits, engines running, on the ramp of Whiteman AFB, MO. The aircraft was pre-flighted prior to its departure for a combat mission in support of Operation Iraqi Freedom on March 21, 2003. *Air Force/509th BW*

BOTTOM RIGHT: B-2 *Spirit of Ohio*, AV-5 (82-1070), sits on the ramp at Nellis AFB, NV, on October 28, 2003. *Spirit of Ohio* and several personnel from Whiteman were sent on temporary duty to Nellis to maintain the aircraft participating in Red Flag 04-01. *Air Force/509th BW*

TOP: Christmas comes early to the maintainers of the B-2A as they walk the partially dismantled B-2A Spirit to the LO dock. Under closer observation, it is evident that this B-2A is in need of a lot of work. To make sure the B-2A doesn't go where it's not wanted, two ground personnel pull along tire chocks. *Air Force/509th BW*

BOTTOM: A view from both sides of the B-2A as it towed through the newly falling snow. What is interesting in this photo is the internal structural pattern that is visible, as the snow fails to sticks to the parts of the skin that are attached to the structure. *Air Force/509th BW*

TOP: Two B-2s, the *Spirit of Ohio*, AV-5 (82-1070), and the *Spirit of California*, AV-9 (88-0330), line up for takeoff on June 29, 2009, on Whiteman's main runway. *Air Force/509th BW*

MIDDLE: Four B-2A Spirit bombers are being recovered on the ramp at Nellis Air Force Base, NV, on October 18, 2003. The bombers are from the 509th Bomb Wing at Whiteman Air Force Base, MO. *Air Force/509th BW*

BOTTOM: B-2 Spirits are being recovered on the ramp at Nellis Air Force Base, NV, on October 18, 2003. The B-2As are from the 509th Bomb Wing at Whiteman AFB, and were sent on temporary duty to Nellis with a cadre of support and maintenance personnel to participate in Exercise Red Flag 04-01. Red Flags are war exercises that allow combat aircrews training in the most realistic simulated war environment possible. *Air Force/509th BW*

The Spirit Arrives in Guam

THE SPIRIT ARRIVES IN GUAM

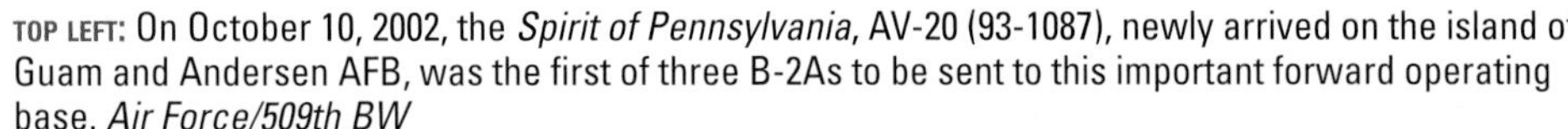

TOP LEFT: On October 10, 2002, the *Spirit of Pennsylvania*, AV-20 (93-1087), newly arrived on the island of Guam and Andersen AFB, was the first of three B-2As to be sent to this important forward operating base. *Air Force/509th BW*

BOTTOM LEFT: A B-2A taxis into place on the flight line at Andersen AFB, Guam, on September 17, 2003, after an eighteen-hour flight from its home at Whiteman AFB. Two B-2As and about 100 airmen from the 509th Bomb Wing were at Andersen AFB for a bomber training exercise. Andersen is a forward-operating location for bombers and is a key player in the Air Force's global power projection. *Air Force/509th BW*

TOP RIGHT: The B-2A *Spirit of Florida*, AV-17 (92-0700), taxis onto the flight line at Andersen Air Force Base AFB, Guam, in support of exercise Coronet Bugle 49. In the foreground is a Dyess-based B-1B Lancer. *Air Force/509th BW*

MIDDLE RIGHT: A B-2A taxis onto the flight line at Andersen AFB, Guam, in support of exercise Coronet Bugle 49. The B-2As are deployed to Andersen from Whiteman AFB, MO. In the background are two B-52H Stratofortresses from Barksdale, AFB, LA. *Air Force/509th BW*

BOTTOM RIGHT: B-2A, the *Spirit of Indiana*, AV-4 (82-1069), lands at Andersen AFB, Guam, on Sunday, April 30, 2006. B-2As replaced the B-1B Lancers at Andersen as part of the continuous bomber rotation. *Air Force/509th BW*

TOP LEFT: A B-2A Spirit, F-15 Eagles, F-16 Fighting Falcons, F/A-18 Hornets, and Japanese P-3 Orion's line the flight line at Andersen Air Force Base, Guam, for Exercise Valiant Shield on June 22, 2006. The exercise concluded on June 23, 2006, and focused on integrated joint training in a variety of mission scenarios. *Air Force/509th BW*

BOTTOM LEFT: A view from the tower at Andersen AFB, Guam, of the *Spirit of Indiana*, AV-4 (82-1069), standing guard with two Boeing B-52Hs (61-0006 and 60-0008), from Barksdale AFB, LA. *Air Force/509th BW*

TOP RIGHT: Two B-2As and four F-15E Strike Eagles are parked inside Hangar 1 at Andersen Air Force Base, Guam, August 6, 2002. The aircraft were moved into the hangar in preparation for a tropical storm that was expected to reach Guam that day. This was the first time the six aircraft had been parked in the hangar, proving to base officials that the hangar could accommodate the aircraft, and aiding in future tropical storm and typhoon planning. The two bombers are deployed with the 13th Expeditionary Bomb Squadron from the 509th Bomb Wing at Whiteman AFB, MO. The fighters are deployed with the 90th Expeditionary Fighter Squadron from the 3rd Wing at Elmendorf AFB, AK. *Air Force/509th BW*

BOTTOM RIGHT: An aerial view of the revetments at Andersen AFB, Guam, with three Boeing B-52H Stratofortress (a.k.a. the 'BUFF') from Barksdale AFB, LA, and three B-2A Spirits from Whitman AFB, MO. During the war in Vietnam, Boeing B-52s of various types were wingtip to wingtip, parking on every available space that could support the weight of the 488,000-pound aircraft. *Air Force/509th BW*

Inside the LO Maintenance Dock

The *Spirit of Alaska*, AV-15 (90-0040), waits its turn in the LO, or Low Observable Maintenance Hangar at Whiteman AFB, MO. *James C. Goodall*

TOP: SrA Wesley Martinez, 509th Maintenance Squadron egress technician, removes screws from the mission commander hatch during a routine inspection August 12, 2014, at Whiteman Air Force Base, MO. The hatches must be removed for inspections on the ACES II ejection seats to ensure serviceability. *Air Force/509th BW*

BOTTOM LEFT: The *Spirit of Pennsylvania*, AV-20 (93-1087), was almost totally dismantled during this photo shoot. They had the escape hatches removed from above the ejection seats, the engine access bay doors were open, as was almost every removable panel on this B-2. The security NCOIC and my escort would let me observe, but not take photographs. In total, security erased thirty-one of the photos I had taken in the LO hangar. *James C. Goodall*

BOTTOM CENTER: A LO technician inspects every inch of the B-2A to ensure that there are no "hot spots" that could give the location of the aircraft. The maintenance crews use a flashlight. A special orange depth gauge is used to determine what area of the B-2A's very sensitive skin needs attention. As in the next photo, all LO work is done in a completely enclosed environment, as the solvents used on stealth coatings are very toxic. *James C. Goodall*

BOTTOM RIGHT: Airmen with the 36th Expeditionary Aircraft Maintenance Squadron sand off degraded paint coatings on a B-2A Spirit at Andersen Air Force Base, Guam. The aircraft was restored once new paint coatings were applied. The plastic tent is used to contain the sanding dust created while removing the paint coatings. *Air Force/509th BW*

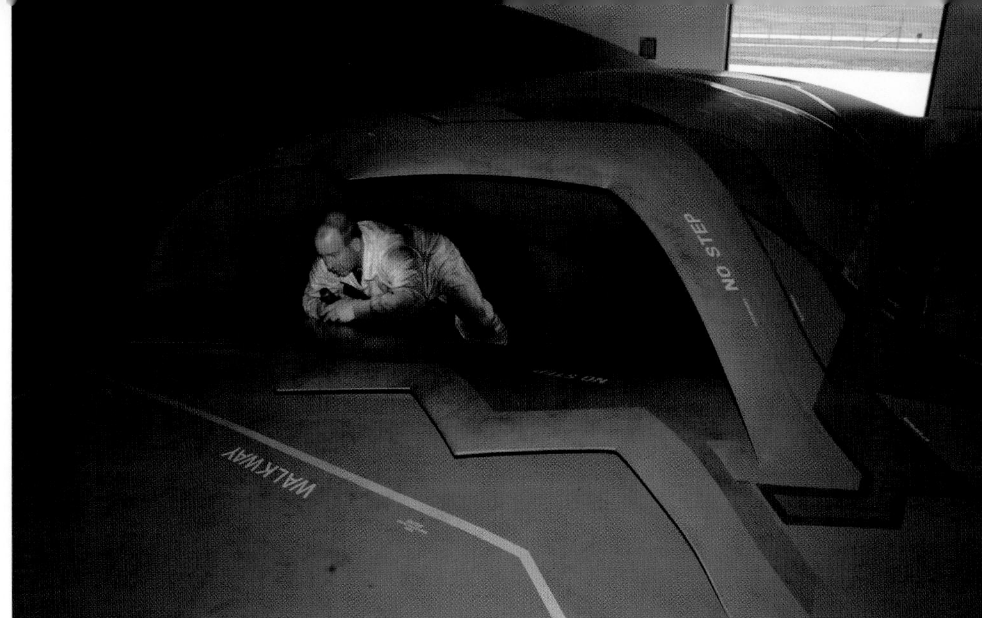

TOP LEFT: SrA Scott Kures, 509th Aircraft Maintenance Squadron, is the crew chief of the *Spirit of* Pennsylvania, AV-20 (93-1087). Here he reviews forms before maintenance is performed on the aircraft October 24, 2007. *Air Force/509th BW*

TOP RIGHT: TSgt Steve Verner climbs out of the engine inlet of his B-2A the *Spirit of Missouri*, AV-8 ((88-0329), after performing post-flight checks at Whiteman Air Force Base on March 22, 2003. The Bomber had just returned from a combat mission over Iraq in support of Operation Iraqi Freedom. *Air Force/509th BW*

BOTTOM LEFT AND RIGHT: With all of the *Spirit of Pennsylvania* access panels open, the B-2A needed to be supported in an extreme way. The B-2A is a rigid airframe and does not flex the way other large aircraft do, so it is imperative to support the aircraft in such a way as to not allow the airframe to flex. *James C. Goodall*

TOP LEFT: In their sealed enclosure, these LO technicians apply new coatings to the bottom of the *Spirit of Alaska*, AV-15 (90-0040), in the LO maintenance hangar at Whiteman on June 3, 2014. *James C. Goodall*

TOP RIGHT: The *Spirit of Pennsylvania*, AV-20 (93-1087), is undergoing an extreme look-over identifying all the areas on the aircraft that require attention from the LO technicians. The metal foil seen in and around the B-2A is to protect newly applied coatings that are in the curing process. *James C. Goodall*

BOTTOM: SrA Alexander Ramirez, 509th MXS Low Observable aircraft structural maintainer, inspects thin tape in the B-2A Spirit's air refueling door at Whiteman Air Force Base, MO, on June 12, 2014. If the tape reaches a certain point of negligible damage, it must be removed and replaced. *Air Force/509th BW*

THE SPIRIT FAMILY TREE

The Spirit Family Tree

The *Spirit of America*, AV-1 (82-1066), was rolled out at Air Force Plant t42 on October 22, 1988; its first flight was July 17, 1989. Before being christened the *Spirit of America*, she was called *Fatal Beauty*. AV-1 was officially named *Spirit of America* and delivered to the USAF on July 14, 2000. *Don Logan*

TOP LEFT: The *Spirit of America*, AV-1, in its dedicated hangar on June 3, 2014. *James C. Goodall*

TOP RIGHT: The *Spirit of America* on landing approach at Whiteman AFB on October 6, 2004. *Don Logan*

MIDDLE RIGHT: The *Spirit of America* during an early morning photo shoot at Air Force Plant 42, Site 4, the home of the B-2's former production facility and now the B-2A's dedicated depot, repair and modification center location. *Northrop Grumman*

BOTTOM RIGHT: The *Spirit of America* touches down on the Nellis runway for an up-coming Red Flag exercise in the spring of 2004. *Don Logan*

The *Spirit of Arizona*, AV-2 (82-1067), is about to touch down on the Nellis runway. Early in its flying carrier, AV-2 was called the "Ship from Hell," because everything that could go wrong did. Its first flight was on October 19, 1989. The *Spirit of Arizona* was named and delivered to USAF on December 7, 1997. *Don Logan*

TOP: The *Spirit of Arizona,* sporting twelve mission markings on its nose gear door, taxis by on April 8, 2014, at Whiteman AFB, MO. *Air Force/509th BW*

BOTTOM LEFT: The *Spirit of Arizona* does a low-level flyby as it leaves Nellis AFB after the conclusion of Red Flag 04-1. *Air Force/509th BW*

BOTTOM RIGHT: *Spirit of Arizona* taxis down to the runway during the rapid launch portion of Global Thunder 12 on October 25, 2011. Global Thunder is designed to exercise all mission areas with primary emphasis on Command and Control. *Air Force/509th BW*

Using B-2A call sign Spirit 01, the *Spirit of New York* is photographed returning to Fairfield RAF Base from a familiarization sortie in and around UK airspace. Its first flight was on June 18, 1991, and early on it was called "The Ghost." It was named *Spirit of New York* on October 10, 1997, but stayed on at Edwards AFB, CA, for flight-testing upgrades to the B-2A fleet. *Author's collection*

TOP LEFT: The *Spirit of New York,* AV-3 (82-1068), arriving at RAF Fairford on July 6, 2012, in very wet, and typical English weather conditions. This was on the eve of RIAT 2012. *Mark McEwan*

BOTTOM LEFT: A good side view of the *Spirit of New York* as it leaves the UK at the conclusion of RIAT-2012 for a flight back to the US and its home at Whiteman AFB, MO. *Air Force/509th BW*

RIGHT: The *Spirit of New York* takes off from Fairford RAF Base for its flight back to Whiteman AFB, MO. Its leaving marked the end of RIAT-2012. *Air Force/509th BW*

The *Spirit of Indiana*, AV-4 (82-1069), on landing approach at Barksdale AFB, LA. AV-4 had the nickname of "Christine" during early flight-test days because some crewmembers thought it was possessed. AV-4's first flight was on April 17, 1992, and it was named and delivered to the Air Force on May 22, 1992. *Author's collection*

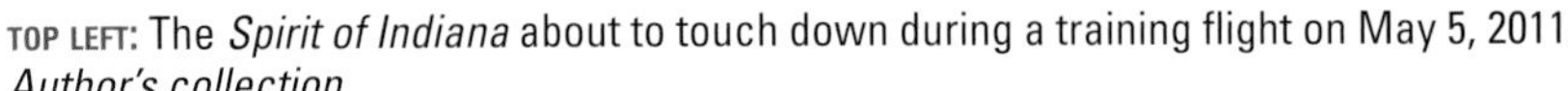

TOP LEFT: The *Spirit of Indiana* about to touch down during a training flight on May 5, 2011. *Author's collection*

TOP RIGHT: The *Spirit of Indiana* approaches the Whiteman runway after a June 13, 2014, training flight. *Air Force/509th BW*

MIDDLE RIGHT: Looking down on the *Spirit of Indiana* as it flies over the central Missouri countryside. *Air Force/509th BW*

BOTTOM RIGHT: The *Spirit of Indiana* from Whiteman AFB, MO, taxis down the runway at RAF Fairford, England, on June 8, 2014. *Air Force/509th BW*

The *Spirit of Ohio*, AV-5 (82-1070), on the taxiway at Whiteman AFB, MO, on October 6, 2004, after participating in a multi-aircraft training sortie. Prior to being named the *Spirit of Ohio*, AV-5 carried the name "Fire & Ice" as it was used for extreme climate testing. The first flight for AV-5 was October 6, 1992, and it was named and delivered to the USAF on July 18, 1997. *Don Logan*

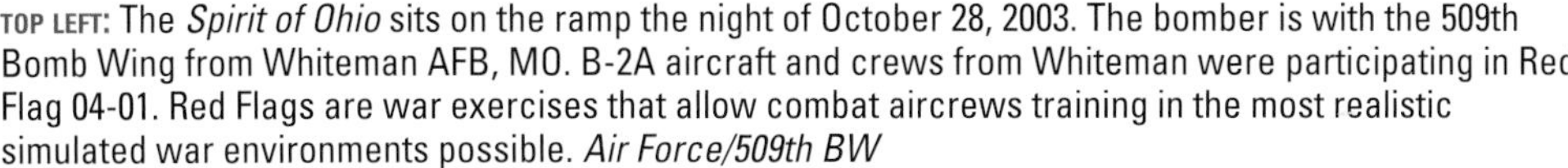
TOP LEFT: The *Spirit of Ohio* sits on the ramp the night of October 28, 2003. The bomber is with the 509th Bomb Wing from Whiteman AFB, MO. B-2A aircraft and crews from Whiteman were participating in Red Flag 04-01. Red Flags are war exercises that allow combat aircrews training in the most realistic simulated war environments possible. *Air Force/509th BW*

TOP RIGHT: The *Spirit of Ohio* lifts off from the Nellis AFB main runway on October 30, 2003, during Red Flag 04-01. *Air Force/509th BW*

MIDDLE RIGHT: The fifth B-2A built, the *Spirit of Ohio* flies overhead for a good bottom view. The split ailerons indicate that this B-2A is in a landing configuration. *Author's collection*

BOTTOM RIGHT: The *Spirit of Ohio* takes off during a Nuclear Operational Readiness Exercise, August 29, 2012, at Whiteman Air Force Base, MO. AV-4 was one of four jets generated and launched for the exercise. *Air Force/509th BW*

The *Spirit of Mississippi*, AV-6 (82-1071), taxis down the Whiteman ramp on April 9, 2014, during a routine training flight. AV-6 was known as the "Black Widow" prior to being named the *Spirit of Mississippi*. Its first flight was on February 2, 1993, and it was named and delivered to the 509th Bomb Wing on May 23, 1998. *Air Force/509th BW*

TOP: Beasts on the prowl. Two B-2s, the *Spirit of Mississippi* and a second B-2A to the rear, taxi down Whiteman's expansive ramp on May 12, 2009. *Air Force/509th BW*

MIDDLE LEFT: The *Spirit of Mississippi* on the taxiway on the British Protectorate or British Indian Ocean Territory, the Island of Diego Garcia, during combat missions over Iraq and Afghanistan. *Air Force/509th BW*

BOTTOM RIGHT: The cockpit of a B-2A *Spirit of Mississippi* as it taxis during the "Beast Walk" during the Nuclear Operation Readiness Exercise, on September 29, 2009. During the exercise, they fly in multiple aircraft to show the 509th Bomb Wing's surety in these tasks. *Air Force/509th BW*

BOTTOM LEFT: The *Spirit of Mississippi* sails into the sky during a training sortie at Whiteman Air Force Base, MO, on July 25, 2013. The revolutionary blending of low-observable technologies with high aerodynamic efficiency and large payload gives the B-2A important advantages over existing bombers. *Air Force/509th BW*

The *Spirit of Texas*, AV-7 (88-0328), on final during a training flight on February 12, 2010. Prior to being named the *Spirit of Texas*, it was known as the "Pirate Ship" and was leased back to Northrop Grumman for electromagnetic compatibility and emission security testing. The first flight was on February 2, 1993, and it was named and delivered to the 509th Bomb Wing on August 31, 1994. *Air Force/509th BW*

TOP: Col. Garrett Harencak, 509th Bomb Wing commander, and Lt. Col. Kevin Ward, 509th BW director of staff, perform a "touch and go" in the *Spirit of Texas* on November 9, 2007. *Air Force/509th BW*

BOTTOM LEFT: *Spirit of Texas* takes to the air for a Red Flag 14-01 mission. This seems to be one of the more rarely seen B-2As. *Author's collection*

BOTTOM RIGHT: Captains William Pogue and Luke Lucero of the 13th Bomb Squadron taxi the *Spirit of Texas* during the "Beast Walk," as part of the Nuclear Operation Readiness Exercise, on September 29, 2009. The NORE is in preparation of the Nuclear Operational Readiness Inspection. *Air Force/509th BW*

Spirit of Missouri takes off for a mission during an air and space expeditionary force deployment to Guam. B-2As were deployed here on February 25, 2005, to provide US Pacific Command officials a continuous bomber presence in the Asia-Pacific region. Its first flight was on September 20, 1993, and was delivered to the 509th Bomb Wing on December 17, 1993. *Air Force/509th BW*

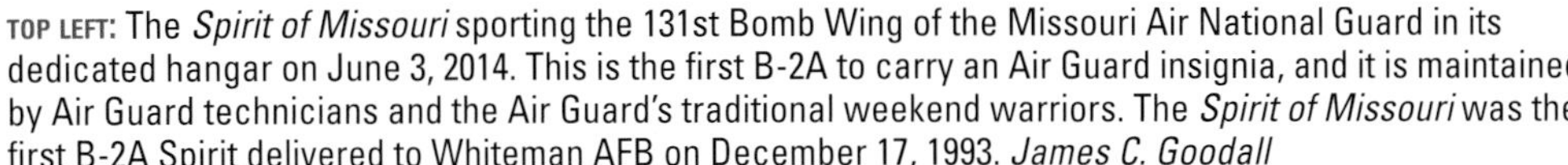

TOP LEFT: The *Spirit of Missouri* sporting the 131st Bomb Wing of the Missouri Air National Guard in its dedicated hangar on June 3, 2014. This is the first B-2A to carry an Air Guard insignia, and it is maintained by Air Guard technicians and the Air Guard's traditional weekend warriors. The *Spirit of Missouri* was the first B-2A Spirit delivered to Whiteman AFB on December 17, 1993. *James C. Goodall*

TOP RIGHT: The *Spirit of Missouri*, AV-8 (88-0329), landing at Nellis AFB, NV, on February 27, 2013, for Red Flag 13-1. Its first flight was on September 20, 1993, and it was delivered to the 509th Bomb Wing on December 17, 1993. *Don Logan*

MIDDLE RIGHT: A beautiful air-to-air view of the *Spirit of Missouri* as it flies over the Missouri countryside. *Don Logan*

BOTTOM RIGHT: Maintenance personnel of the 509th Aircraft Maintenance Squadron recover the *Spirit of Missouri* prior to being towed into its hangar on March 22, 2003. The bomber had just returned from a combat mission over Iraq in support of Operation Iraqi Freedom, in which it flew half way around the world. *Air Force/509th BW*

The *Spirit of California*, AV-9 (88-0330), takes off during a base exercise on April 9, 2014, at Whiteman AFB, MO. Its first flight was on January 25, 1994, and was delivered to the 509th Bomb Wing on March 31, 1994. AV-9 was the second B-2A delivered. *Air Force/509th BW*

TOP: Two F-15E Strike Eagles and the *Spirit of California* in formation over Anderson AFB, Guam. The Strike Eagles are with the 391st Expeditionary Fighter Squadron from Mountain Home AFB, ID. The *Spirit of California* is from the 325th Expeditionary Bomb Squadron from Whiteman AFB, MO. *Air Force/509th BW*

BOTTOM LEFT: The *Spirit of California* does a flyby showing a nice top view of the beast. The first time you see a B-2A in the air it really does take your breath away. In some ways it looks small, that is until you get up-close and personal. It is a big airplane. *Air Force/509th BW*

BOTTOM RIGHT: The *Spirit of California* takes off on an overcast day while participating in Red Flag, February 5, 2009. Red Flag is an advanced aerial combat training exercise hosted at Nellis AFB, NV. About 100 members of Team Whiteman participated in Red Flag for the two-week long, large force exercise that included more than eighty-five aircraft from the US and Britain. *Air Force/509th BW*

The *Spirit of South Carolina*, AV-10 (88-0331), taxis down the Whiteman flight line prior to takeoff, August 22, 2009. Twenty B-2A bombers are assigned to the 509th Bomb Wing. The B-2A brings massive firepower to bear, in a short time, anywhere on the globe and through previously impenetrable defenses. Its first flight was on April 26, 1994, and it was delivered to the 509th Bomb Wing and named *Spirit of South Carolina* on April 15, 1995. *Air Force/509th BW*

TOP LEFT: The *Spirit of South Carolina* in its dedicated hangar. On the floor of the hangar, note the number of round metal disks; these are where fire suppression foam comes out if there is a flash fire. *Air Force/509th BW*

TOP RIGHT: Another view of the *Spirit of South Carolina* on final approach during a "Touch-and-Go" at Whiteman on June 24, 2014. *Air Force/509th BW*

BOTTOM RIGHT: The *Spirit of South Carolina* on a landing approach to Whiteman on May 20, 2011. *Air Force/509th BW*

The *Spirit of Washington* lands at Whiteman AFB, MO, December 16, 2013. The *Spirit of Washington* participated in its first training mission here after an engine fire in 2010 badly damaged the aircraft. The *Spirit of Washington* was preparing to fly a mission at Andersen AFB, Guam, when one of its four engines caught fire. After nearly four years and around $60 million (USD), the aircraft was restored to full mission-ready status. *Air Force/509th BW*

TOP LEFT: The *Spirit of Washington* from Whiteman AFB, MO, is refueled by personnel from the 99th Logistics Readiness Squadron, at Nellis AFB, NV on March 1, 2005. The aircraft is assigned to the 509th Bomb Wing and is participating in a Red Flag exercise at Nellis. *Air Force/509th BW*

TOP RIGHT: The *Spirit of Washington*, AV-11 (88-0332), on the final leg of a training mission lands at Travis AFB, CA. Its first flight was on June 20, 1994, and it was delivered to the 509th Bomb Wing on October 29, 1994. *Air Force/509th BW*

MIDDLE RIGHT: *Spirit of Washington* on final approach to Nellis AFB, NV, to participate in the Air Forces Red Flag 05-01 on March 1, 2005 *Air Force/509th BW*

BOTTOM RIGHT: Maj. Geoffrey J. Romanowicz, 393rd Bomb Squadron pilot, and Jay Gibson, Assistant Secretary of the Air Force for Financial Management, taxi by the hangars in the *Spirit of Washington*, May 22, 2008. *Air Force/509th BW*

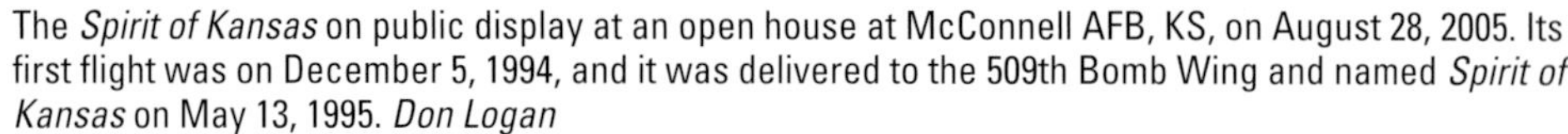

The *Spirit of Kansas* on public display at an open house at McConnell AFB, KS, on August 28, 2005. Its first flight was on December 5, 1994, and it was delivered to the 509th Bomb Wing and named *Spirit of Kansas* on May 13, 1995. *Don Logan*

LEFT: This is what $2.2 billion dollars look like after a loss of control due to mechanical problems with moisture in the static ports. The *Spirit of Kansas* crashed at Anderson AFB, Guam, on February 23, 2008. The *Spirit of* Kansas accumulated 5,176 flight hours on 1,036 sorties prior to the loss. It is important to note that the ejection seats worked as designed and the crew ejected safely. *Author's collection*

TOP RIGHT: A B-2, the *Spirit of Kansas*, deployed from Whiteman AFB, MO, began flying operations October 16, 2007, at Andersen AFB, Guam. The stealth bomber airmen deployed here were fully integrated with the rest of the 36th Wing to take full advantage of integrated training opportunities. *Air Force/509th BW*

BOTTOM RIGHT: The *Spirit of Kansas*, AV-12 (89-0127), taxis on the Whiteman ramp the summer of 2005. Its first flight was on December 5, 1994, and it was delivered to the 509th Bomb Wing on February 17, 1995. It was named on May 13, 1995. *Author's collection*

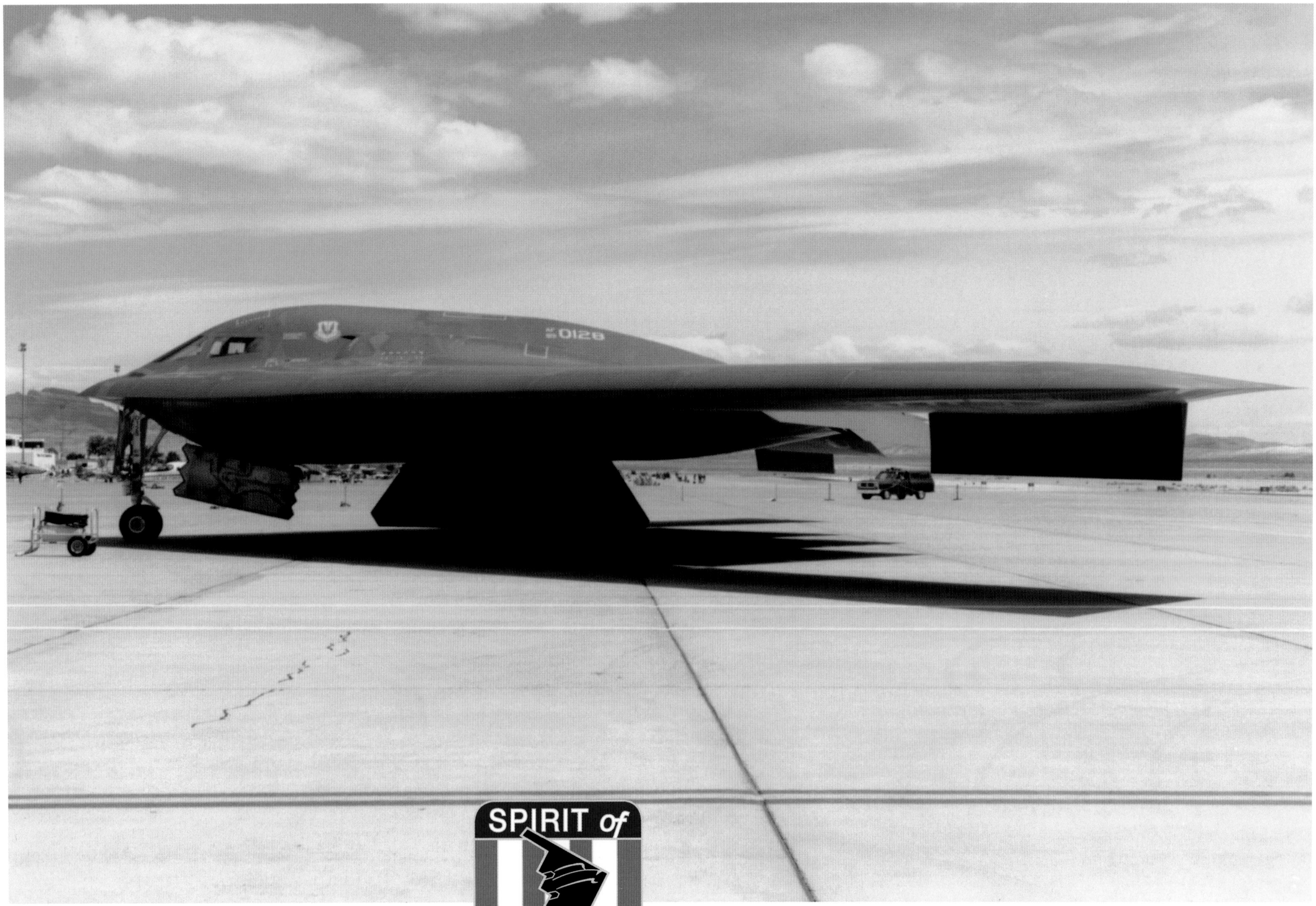

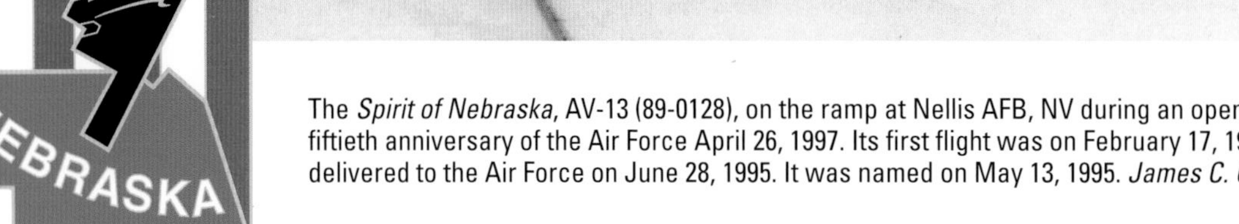

The *Spirit of Nebraska*, AV-13 (89-0128), on the ramp at Nellis AFB, NV during an open house marking the fiftieth anniversary of the Air Force April 26, 1997. Its first flight was on February 17, 1995, and it was delivered to the Air Force on June 28, 1995. It was named on May 13, 1995. *James C. Goodall*

TOP LEFT: The *Spirit of Nebraska* on the ramp at Nellis AFB, NV, during an open house marking the fiftieth anniversary of the USAF, April 26, 1997. In this photo, the Block 20 Leading Edge clips are very visible. *James C. Goodall*

BOTTOM LEFT: A beautiful sight as the *Spirit of Nebraska* does a banking turn during a flyby at Whiteman AFB, MO, on May 19, 2012. *Author's collection*

TOP RIGHT: Canada's Aerial Demonstration Team, the Snowbirds perform, banking right in full formation, smoke trailing high above the *Spirit of Nebraska* at Nellis AFB during the USAF's fiftieth anniversary and airshow on April 26, 1997. *Air Force/509th BW*

BOTTOM RIGHT: This view of the *Spirit of Nebraska* is one of my favorite close-up shots of the B-2A showing all of the different shades of blue-gray. It almost looks like it is one of the camouflage patterns Keith Ferris is famous for. *Author's collection*

The *Spirit of Georgia*, AV-14 (89-0129), as it does a low level flyby during San Francisco's "Fleet Week" on October 6, 2012. Its first flight was on July 6, 1995, and it was delivered to the 509th Bomb Wing on November 14, 1995, as a Block 10 B-2. It was upgraded to Block 20 status in March of 1997, and delivered back to the 509th BW as a Block 30 B-2A in 1999. *Author's collection*

TOP LEFT: The *Spirit of Georgia* taxis alongside the main runway on the island of Diego Garcia while a B-52H from Barksdale AFB lands alongside her. *Air Force/509th BW*

TOP RIGHT: Two B-2s, the *Spirit of Georgia* and the *Spirit of America*, AV-1 (82-1066), from the 509th Wing at Whiteman AFB, taxi onto the parking ramp at Andersen AFB, Guam, on February 23, 2009. More than 250 airmen and six B-2A Spirits, deployed from Whiteman AFB, MO, and began arriving here on February 23, 2009 to replace the 23rd Expeditionary Bomb Squadron, and its B-52H Stratofortresses as the Pacific region's continuous US bomber presence. *Air Force/509th BW*

BOTTOM RIGHT: SSgt Kyle Helton marshals *Spirit of Georgia,* while A1C Patrick Holter places chocks on February 23, 2009, after arriving at Andersen AFB, Guam. *Air Force/509th BW*

The Spirit of Alaska, AV-15 (90-0040), on a landing approach to Whiteman AFB, MO during a touch-and-go landing practice. *The Spirit of Alaska's* first flight was on August 28, 1995, was delivered to the Air Force on January 24, 1996, and named on June 27, 1996. *Author's collection*

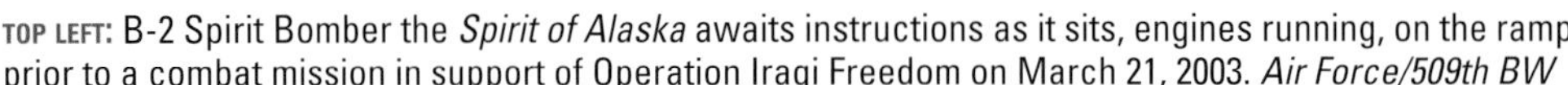

TOP LEFT: B-2 Spirit Bomber the *Spirit of Alaska* awaits instructions as it sits, engines running, on the ramp prior to a combat mission in support of Operation Iraqi Freedom on March 21, 2003. *Air Force/509th BW*

TOP RIGHT: A1C Joshua Anderson waits to signal the pilot of the *Spirit of Alaska* to taxi the aircraft on the ramp on October 23, 2003. Anderson is a crew chief from the 509th Aircraft Maintenance Squadron at Whiteman AFB, MO. He is responsible for keeping the bomber mission ready by ensuring that all required maintenance is completed for a Red Flag exercise. *Air Force/509th BW*

MIDDLE RIGHT: The *Spirit of Alaska* stands ready in its dedicated hangar during exercise Global Guardian. Inside pilots are seen climbing into their seats and discussing maintenance items with crew chief before engines are started. This close-up shows the Block 20 leading edge configuration with the clips on the seams of the leading edge. *Air Force/509th BW*

BOTTOM RIGHT: Looking down the leading edge of the *Spirit of Alaska* as it prepares for takeoff during Global Guardian. If you look closely, the Block 20 clips are visible. *Air Force/509th BW*

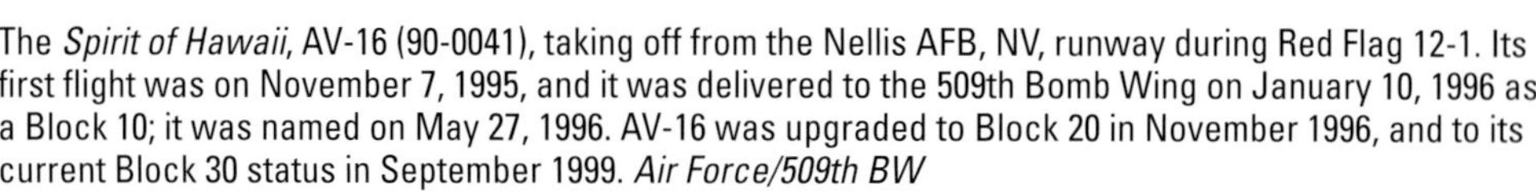

The *Spirit of Hawaii*, AV-16 (90-0041), taking off from the Nellis AFB, NV, runway during Red Flag 12-1. Its first flight was on November 7, 1995, and it was delivered to the 509th Bomb Wing on January 10, 1996 as a Block 10; it was named on May 27, 1996. AV-16 was upgraded to Block 20 in November 1996, and to its current Block 30 status in September 1999. *Air Force/509th BW*

TOP LEFT: The *Spirit of Hawaii* taxies around the flight line at Whiteman AFB, MO, during the 509th Bomb Wing's first "Beast Walk" Exercise. "Beast Walk" is a nuclear alert exercise in which the bombers respond using quick engine start and taxi procedures. *Author's collection*

TOP RIGHT: The *Spirit of Hawaii* taxis down the Nellis AFB, NV, runway after a day of flying during Red Flag 12-01. *Author's collection*

BOTTOM RIGHT: *Spirit of Hawaii* taxis at Whiteman AFB, MO, June 1, 2013. Onboard, pilot Lt. Col. Michael Means, 131st Bomb Wing, Missouri Air National Guard, is on his final flight before retirement. Means holds the B-2A flying hours record for the Air National Guard with 1,765.8 hours, and is ranked second of both active and guard pilots. *Air Force/509th BW*

The *Spirit of Florida*, AV-17 (92-0700), was delivered as a Block 20 B-2A to the 509th Bomb Wing on July 3, 1996, and was named on October 23, 1996. The *Spirit of Florida* was upgraded to its current Block 30 status in December 1999. Its first flight was on February 10, 1996, and it was named and delivered to the 509th Bomb Wing on October 23, 1996. *Don Logan*

TOP LEFT: The B-2A the *Spirit of Florida* flown by Lt. Col. Brian Copello, mission commander, and Capt. John Avery, pilot, taxis to the runway April 17. In the background, the *Spirit of Louisiana*, AV-21 (93-1088), flown by Lt. Col. Frank Cavuoti, mission commander, and Capt. Todd Moenster, pilot, follows directly after. The B-2A returned to flying April 15, 2008, following a fifty-three-day safety pause, after the first-ever crash on February 23, 2008 in Guam. *Air Force/509th BW*

TOP RIGHT: The *Spirit of Florida*'s first flight was on February 10, 1996. Since it first arrived at Whiteman AFB in July 1996, its stealthiness and massive firepower have been used in missions around the world. During its mission on April 1, 2013, the aircraft and its crew celebrated a monumental milestone as it became the first B-2A Spirit to surpass 7,000 flight hours. *Air Force/509th BW*

MIDDLE RIGHT: B-2 *Spirit of Florida* takes off on the runway October 26, 2012. Its capability to penetrate air defenses and threaten effective retaliation provides a strong, effective deterrent and combat force well into the twenty-first century. *Air Force/509th BW*

BOTTOM RIGHT: The B-2A, *Spirit of Florida* lands at Whiteman AFB, MO, on April 1, 2013. The pilots just completed a historic training mission in which it became the first B-2A to reach 7,000 flight hours. *Don Logan*

The *Spirit of Oklahoma*, AV-18 (93-1085), takes off from Andersen AFB, Guam, on March 30, 2005. Six B-2A Spirits and more than 270 personnel from the 393rd Bomb Squadron at Whiteman Air Force Base, MO, were deployed here in support of Pacific Command's continuous bomber presence in the Asia–Pacific region. Its first flight was on April 11, 1996, and was delivered to the 509th Bomb Wing on May 15, 1996. It was named on September 14, 1996. *Air Force/509th BW*

TOP LEFT: A night shot of the Whiteman ramp as the *Spirit of Oklahoma* prepares to leave for Andersen AFB, Guam on March 17, 2004. *Air Force/509th BW*

TOP RIGHT: The *Spirit of Oklahoma* does a banking flyby for the ground crew on temporary to Andersen AFB, Guam, on March 30, 2005. *Air Force/509th BW*

MIDDLE RIGHT: The *Spirit of Oklahoma* flies in formation with a Barksdale Boeing B-52H (60-0050) on a flyby on September 17, 2003, after an eighteen-hour flight from its home at Whiteman AFB, MO. Two B-2As and about 100 airmen from the 509th Bomb Wing were at Andersen, AFB for a bomber training exercise. *Air Force/509th BW*

BOTTOM RIGHT: On November 22, 2004, after flying halfway around the world, just barely visible in the upper right hand corner of the photo, is the temporary home for the *Spirit of Oklahoma* while assigned to temporary duty on the remote Indian Ocean island of Diego Garcia. *Air Force/509th BW*

The *Spirit of Kitty Hawk*, AV-19 (93-1086), on the tarmac at Whiteman AFB, MO, on May 7, 2011, and being pre-flighted for a training mission later in the day. Its first flight was on August 1, 1996, and it was delivered to the 509th Bomb Wing on August 30, 1996; it was named on December 16, 1996. The *Spirit of Kitty Hawk* was returned to Northrop for upgrade to Block 30, and returned to flight in January 2000. *Air Force/509th BW*

TOP: The *Spirit of Kitty Hawk* at rest on the ramp of the 509th Bomb Wing on June 3, 2014, while maintenance crews work on some problems with the port landing gear. *James C. Goodall*

BOTTOM LEFT: The *Spirit of Kitty Hawk* does a flyby as a result of a required maintenance flight to validate the work performed on the Spirit's navigation systems. *Air Force/509th BW*

BOTTOM RIGHT: The *Spirit of Kitty Hawk* on landing approach to Nellis AFB, NV, after a day participating in Red Flag 12-1. *Air Force/509th BW*

The *Spirit of Pennsylvania*, AV-20 (93-1087), returns to Whiteman AFB, MO, on March 20, 2011, after a training mission over the Utah Training and Bombing range. Its first flight was on April 15, 1997, and it was delivered to the 509th Bomb Wing on August 5, 1997; it was named on the same day. The *Spirit of Pennsylvania* was delivered new as a Block 30 B-2A. *Air Force/509th BW*

TOP LEFT: Its been rumored that the B-2A uses its massive landing gear doors as vertical tails during low speed flying such as on takeoff. Here is a perfect example of the *Spirit of Pennsylvania* with landing gear fully retracted, and the gear doors are still fully extended. *Air Force/509th BW*

TOP RIGHT: The *Spirit of Pennsylvania* undergoes a thorough checkout after maintenance crews replaced several critical systems. *Air Force/509th BW*

MIDDLE RIGHT: The *Spirit of Pennsylvania* heads out for an evening low-level training mission on June 23, 2014. *Air Force/509th BW*

BOTTOM RIGHT: On the flight line at Andersen AFB, Guam, September 17, 2003, after an eighteen-hour flight from its home at Whiteman AFB, MO, the *Spirit of Pennsylvania* groundcrew are doing a post-flight inspection and a thorough checkout prior to its next flight. Two B-2As and about 100 Airmen from the 509th Bomb Wing were at Andersen AFB for a bomber training exercise. *Air Force/509th BW*

The *Spirit of Louisiana*, AV-21 (93-1088), and the last B-2A built, taxis down the Nellis flight line during a Red Flag exercise. Its first flight was on August 4, 1997, and it was delivered to the 509th Bomb Wing on November 10, 1997; it was named on the same day. *Don Logan*

TOP LEFT: The *Spirit of Louisiana* taxis down the Nellis flight line after a day of flying during a Red Flag exercise. *Don Logan*

TOP RIGHT: This is not something seen very often. Call sign "Death 12" holding, while the *Spirit of Louisiana* as "Death 11," the *Spirit of Arizona*, AV-2 (82-1067), performs an overshoot after arriving at RAF Fairford for a temporary deployment. *Author's collection*

MIDDLE RIGHT: The *Spirit of Louisiana* at Whiteman AFB, MO, on February 24, 2014, circles in for a landing. The B-2A's capability to penetrate air defenses and threaten effective retaliation provides a strong, effective deterrent and combat force well into the twenty-first century. *Air Force/509th BW*

BOTTOM RIGHT: Maintainers and crew chiefs from the 509th Aircraft Maintenance Squadron prepare the *Spirit of Louisiana* on March 19, 2011, at Whiteman Air Force Base, MO, in support of Operation Odyssey Dawn. *Air Force/509th BW*

Keeping the Talons of the Beast Sharp

LEFT: Crew chiefs and maintainers prep a Northrop T-38 Talon prior to flight on Jan. 26, 2011, Whiteman AFB, MO. More than 72,000 US Air Force pilots have trained in Northrop's T-38 Talon, the world's first supersonic trainer when it entered service. Nearly 1,200 Talons were produced from 1961 to 1972, and more than 500 are currently operational with the Air Force and NASA. *Air Force/509th BW*

RIGHT: A Northrop T-38 Talon flies in formation with the B-2A *Spirit of South Carolina*, AV-10 (88-0331), during a training mission over Whiteman Air Force Base, MO, on February 20, 2014. *Air Force/509th BW*

TOP LEFT: With the B-2A a very limited and expensive resource, B-2A pilots still need their required number of flight hours and proficiency training. In order to keep that sharp edge, the pilots of the 509th Bomb Wing fly the Northrop T-38 Talon supersonic trainer. The 394th Training Squadron has a stable of twelve to fourteen of these very sleek jets for the use of the Wing's fliers. *James C. Goodall*

BOTTOM LEFT: In the 1950s, with jets growing larger and more expensive, Northrop developed a design for a small, simple, and inexpensive—yet still supersonic—aircraft. The T-38 Talon is powered by two GE J85 engines weighing less than 500 pounds, yet producing up to 5,000 pounds of thrust. *James C. Goodall*

TOP RIGHT: On most bases that have training or fighter/attack aircraft, at least one is usually dedicated to the wing and/or squadron commanders. At Whiteman AFB, this honor goes to a T-38A that carries "509th BW" on the tail with its serial number (67-0845) in two-inch letters at the base of the tail. *James C. Goodall*

BOTTOM RIGHT: A T-38 Talon from the 509th Bomb Wing is readied for a training sortie at Whiteman AFB, MO, on June 3, 2014. The T-38 Talon is a twin-engine, high-altitude, supersonic jet trainer used in a variety of roles because of its design, economy of operations, ease of maintenance, high performance, and exceptional safety record. *James C. Goodall*

TOP LEFT: From almost any angle the Northrop T-38 Talon is an eye-pleasing design. The aircraft seats two pilots and is powered by two General Electric J-85 jet engines at the wing roots. Its breathtaking performance has earned it the nickname "White Rocket." In 1962, the T-38 set absolute time-to-climb records for 3,000, 6,000, 9,000, and 12,000 meters, beating the records for those altitudes set by the Lockheed F-104 Starfighter in December 1958. *James C. Goodall*

BOTTOM LEFT: T-38 Talon pilots perform their pre-flight inspections prior to take off, January 26, 2011, Whiteman AFB, MO. Every T-38 Talon built by Northrop was delivered on time, at or below the contract price, and with performance as promised. The final T-38 was delivered to the Air Force in 1972. *Air Force/509th BW*

TOP RIGHT: From left: SrA Jacob Duarte; A1C Breanna Mack, both from the 509th Maintenance Squadron; and SSgt Joseph Swanson, 131st Maintenance Squadron, perform a bond master inspection on the critical honeycomb areas of a T-38 Talon at Whiteman AFB, MO, on January 26, 2011. *Air Force/509th BW*

BOTTOM RIGHT: T-38 Talons sit tail-to-tail in a 394th Combat Training Squadron hangar prior to being taxied out for flights, January 26, 2011, Whiteman AFB, MO. *Air Force/509th BW*

Protecting the Beast

TOP LEFT: SrA Richie Madrigal, 509th Security Forces Squadron response force member, provides close bound sentry for a B-2A Spirit, on October 28, 2013. The 509th SFS maintains current defense skills to protect base assets and follow the Air Force Global Strike Command vision of being an elite, highly disciplined team. *Air Force/509th BW*

TOP RIGHT: SSgt Grant Meyers, 509th Security Forces Squadron military working dog trainer, acts as an aggressor as a military working dog bites him, while SSgt Amanda Cubbage, 509th SFS canine handler, supervises during a bite sleeve scenario at Whiteman Air Force Base, April 23, 2013. Bite sleeve scenarios are used to teach the canines controlled aggression and obedience. *Air Force/509th BW*

BOTTOM LEFT: 509th Security Force personnel, Whiteman Air Force Base, MO, take control of M-9 pistols from a B-2A Stealth Bomber Alert Crew involved in a simulated vehicle accident during Global Guardian. *Air Force/509th BW*

BOTTOM CENTER: On June 3, 2014, SSgt Cuevas, with his K9 "Norbo," puts the canine through his paces during a demonstration at the military working dog compound at Whiteman AFB, MO. *James C. Goodall*

BOTTOM RIGHT: 509th Security Force Squadron personnel use their under-vehicle mirror as they inspect vehicles both entering and leaving the priority-A area around the B-2A Spirit and hangars. Although it is conducted during exercise Global Guardian, this is a normal procedure when passing through the Entry Control Point. *Air Force/509th BW*

TOP LEFT: A armored Humvee on the flight line is a typical sight on most military bases post 9/11 as security has risen dramatically. *James C. Goodall*

MIDDLE LEFT: SSgt Cuevas again with "Norbo" demonstrating what the dog can do as it runs through the obstacle course at the military working dogs compound. As beautiful as these creatures are, they are considered military equipment and carry a part number, and are not pets. *James C. Goodall*

BOTTOM LEFT: Two are better than one. Standing in front of the Air Force Reserve hangar at Whiteman AFB, two of the security police's finest stand watch on the flight line to make sure all is secured. *James C. Goodall*

TOP RIGHT: This is the home to the eight to ten working dogs that are assigned to the Whiteman AFB security. Each K9 has its own pen where it spends its off-patrol time. When a handler is reassigned, the dogs stay assigned to the base. During handler change outs, they usually pull the K9 from working duties for about ninety days before a new handler takes over. *James C. Goodall*

BOTTOM CENTER: SSgt Amanda Cubbage, 509th Security Forces Squadron canine handler, holds back her canine, "Mina," during a controlled aggression exercise at Whiteman Air Force Base, March 23, 2013. The exercise teaches canines to follow commands and helps strengthen the bond between dogs and their handlers. *Air Force/509th BW*

BOTTOM RIGHT: During a tour of the base's military working dog kennels on June 3, 2014, SSgt Cuevas with "Norbo" stands proud during a "Show and Tell" at Whiteman AFB, MO. Military working dogs are not pets and the only people allowed to interact with the dogs are their handlers. *James C. Goodall*

The Fathers of the B-2

The fathers of the B-2A Stealth Bomber: Dr. John Cashen, Irv Waaland, and Jim Kinnu. These are the three names on the B-2A patent. *Dr. John Cashen*

Author Bio

Over the past thirty-five years, Jim Goodall has authored over two dozen books and articles on military aircraft, naval ships, and submarines. This book on the Northrop Grumman B-2A Spirit is his twenty-first published work. Goodall is an expert on Lockheed's family of Blackbirds with multiple books on the subject. He also co-authored and published the very first book on the F-117A Stealth fighter with longtime friend, Bill Sweetman. He's written multiple books on Stealth aircraft, photo essays on the US Navy's fleet of Ballistic Missile and Attack Submarines, and on the Nimitz Class CVNs.